YORK NOTES

Heart of Darkness

Joseph Conrad

Notes by Hena Maes-Jelinek

 LONGMAN

 York Press

YORK PRESS
322 Old Brompton Road, London SW5 9JH

Pearson Education Limited
Edinburgh Gate, Harlow,
Essex CM20 2JE, United Kingdom
Associated companies, branches and representatives throughout the world

First published 1998
Fourth impression 2001

ISBN 0-582-32919-1

Designed by Vicki Pacey, Trojan Horse, London
Phototypeset by Gem Graphics, Trenance, Mawgan Porth, Cornwall
Colour reproduction and film output by Spectrum Colour
Produced by Pearson Education North Asia Limited, Hong Kong

CONTENTS

PART ONE

INTRODUCTION

HOW TO STUDY A NOVEL

Studying a novel on your own requires self-discipline and a carefully thought-out work plan in order to be effective.

- You will need to read the novel more than once. Start by reading it quickly for pleasure, then read it slowly and thoroughly.

- On your second reading make detailed notes on the plot, characters and themes of the novel. Further readings will generate new ideas and help you to memorise the details of the story.

- Some of the characters will develop as the plot unfolds. How do your responses towards them change during the course of the novel?

- Think about how the novel is narrated. From whose point of view are events described?

- A novel may or may not present events chronologically: the time-scheme may be a key to its structure and organisation.

- What part do the settings play in the novel?

- Are words, images or incidents repeated so as to give the work a pattern? Do such patterns help you to understand the novel's themes?

- Identify what styles of language are used in the novel.

- What is the effect of the novel's ending? Is the action completed and closed, or left incomplete and open?

- Does the novel present a moral and just world?

- Cite exact sources for all quotations, whether from the text itself or from critical commentaries. Wherever possible find your own examples from the novel to back up your opinions.

- Always express your ideas in your own words.

This York Note offers an introduction to *Heart of Darkness* and cannot substitute close reading of the text and the study of secondary sources.

Heart of Darkness has been called the first modern novel. It is indeed a work of powerful creative imagination which is shown, in retrospect, to have shed a completely new, if rather bleak, light on the West and its civilising mission at the turn of the twentieth century. It was a time of hope when people thought that science and progress would at last bring happiness to humankind. In many ways the novel was ahead of its time when it was first published. If you are familiar with nineteenth-century fiction, you will soon realise how radically Joseph Conrad's story differs from it. He himself knew exactly what he was doing and wrote about it: 'I am *modern,* and I would rather recall Wagner the musician and Rodin the sculptor who both had to starve a little in their day … they had to suffer for being "new"'.

One feature of the nineteenth-century novel is that, although authors did not refrain from criticising the society in which they lived (see Charles Dickens and George Eliot), they did not fundamentally question its order and organisation. Marlow's (and Joseph Conrad's) suggestion that only the policeman and the butcher keep people on the right path in the civilised West (p. 64) and his assertion that when one is hungry, 'principles … are less than chaff in a breeze' (p. 57) may have shocked readers who must have been convinced that their society was the most advanced and progressive in the world and that, as individuals, they were capable of heroic behaviour in any circumstance. *Heart of Darkness* questions the 'meliorism' or belief in one's capacity to progress and improve morally, a belief propounded by George Eliot and her intellectual friends.

By contrast, both in content and form, *Heart of Darkness* throws doubt on all former certainties and in this respect, prefigures later political, philosophical and fictional developments in both life and art. This century has indeed seen the advent of extraordinary scientific and technological progress. Decolonisation has also liberated many subject people(s). But it is, equally, a century replete with conquests, wars and genocides. *Heart of Darkness* brings to light, through Kurtz's behaviour, the motivations behind such devastating conduct: will-to-power and greed for material riches.

Disruptive political events together with scientific discoveries at the beginning of the twentieth century (in psychology, for instance, or Einstein's theory of relativity) were to change the conception of the nature and finality of existence and lead to increasing doubt and uncertainty in practically all fields of experience. This is foreshadowed by Marlow's repeated self-questioning when, removed from so-called civilised society

y

and confronted with an environment he doesn't understand, he starts thinking about humanity's position in the universe. The fact that his questions are never answered and that Kurtz's 'glimpsed truth' ('The horror! The horror!' – p. 86) remains an enigma suggest, as one critic put it, 'the historic predicament of mind-tortured modern Europe' (Said, *Joseph Conrad and the Fiction of Autobiography*, 1966, p. 113). Joseph Conrad's pessimistic portrait of humanity, of its bewilderment and alienation in an unknown universe in *Heart of Darkness* announce the negative vision of a writer like Samuel Beckett (1906–89).

Uncertainty and the sense of relativity implied in Marlow's confrontation with a world very different from his own are also conveyed by the form of the novel. *Heart of Darkness* breaks with the convention of the omniscient narrator who, to a large extent, took for granted the generally accepted view of society that he or she portrayed. You will find that critics disagree about the reliability of Marlow as a narrator. That his narrative should be enclosed in the first narrator's story is a kind of *mise-en-abyme*, an expression which describes the process of telling a story within a story or writing a novel within a novel. *Heart of Darkness* also contains **self-reflexive** comments, that is, comments on its own origin and writing process or, in this case, storytelling. Moreover, when the first narrator says that Marlow's narrative 'seemed to shape itself without human lips' (p. 43), he seems to anticipate the doubt thrown by late-twentieth-century critics on the notion that a literary work is the original creation of an individual writer. Joseph Conrad's language, above all his use of nouns and adjectives, combine to create the uncertainty mentioned above while giving his narrative a deeper, if not always obvious, meaning.

Heart of Darkness is sometimes called a long short story or a novella. But its complexity and inexhaustible richness makes it more akin to a novel. It can be read an unlimited number of times and each new reading is likely to yield new shades of meaning. If you approach it for the first time, you will see that it is a novel about colonialism; you will be able to follow Marlow's journey into the African interior; but you may well ask yourself questions about Marlow's disquisitions on human behaviour and the significance of his meeting with Kurtz. You are advised to read the novel once for pleasure and interest, and a second time with the help of these notes. The subsequent reading(s) will involve a systematic survey of all the elements that make up the form of the novel and cannot be dissociated from its content. Note that what is called below Joseph Conrad's 'associative method' requires the reader's participation to discern the ironic parallels and contrasts by which meaning is conveyed.

One golden rule in literary analysis is never to take for granted another reader's or critic's interpretation of a text. Criticism is meant to help you, not to replace your own thinking. In forming your own opinion, however, always make sure that it is substantiated by the text.

PART TWO

Summaries

Heart of Darkness was first serialised in *Blackwood's Magazine* from February to April 1899, and then in *Living Age* from 18 June to 4 August 1900. It was first published in book form in 1902 together with *Youth* (as the title story) and *The End of the Tether*. It was republished in the Uniform Edition of the *Works of Joseph Conrad* (22 vols., Dent, London, 1923–8) with an Author's Note to each volume. It was reissued in the Collected Edition of the *Works of Joseph Conrad* (Dent, London, 1946–54). There are now many paperback editions of *Heart of Darkness*, which usually include also a selection of representative critical essays. *Heart of Darkness*, A Norton Critical Edition, edited by Robert Kimbrough also contains an extensive section on 'Background and Sources' as well as extracts from Joseph Conrad's non-fictional writings. These Notes refer to pages in the text edited by Ross C. Murfin for the Series 'Case Studies in Contemporary Criticism', Second Edition. Boston/New York: Bedford Books of St Martin's Press, 1996.

Synopsis

In the Thames estuary five men sit on board the *Nellie*, a cruising boat. One is the nameless first narrator of the novel, who introduces his four companions: there is the Director of Companies (their captain and host); a lawyer; an accountant; and finally Marlow, a seaman who, in several works by Joseph Conrad, relates his experiences or, as in *Lord Jim*, comments on the adventurous life of another man. While they are waiting for the tide to turn, Marlow tells the others of an experience he once had in Africa.

As a child Marlow was fascinated by the River Congo (unnamed in the story). His childhood dream materialised when he obtained the command of a steamboat to travel up that river. He first went to Brussels (also unnamed) to visit the headquarters of the company that sponsored his journey. The death-like atmosphere of the city and of the company headquarters, together with the weird behaviour of the people he met there, seemed to him ominous signs. He was, moreover, made uncomfortable by the realisation that he was looked upon as an emissary of light. His uneasiness grew during the journey to Africa, which gave him a first glimpse into the colonialist enterprise. Marlow's suspicions were confirmed on reaching the first or Outer Station on the river. His first view was of black men made to work for an apparently useless purpose, or being too weak to work and simply left to die. Marlow's horror was matched only by his surprise when he saw a white man, the company's chief accountant, elegantly and meticulously attired, clearly unaware of, or indifferent to, the surroundings in which he kept the company's books 'in apple-pie order' (p. 33). The accountant was the first to tell Marlow about Kurtz, the first-class agent he would meet in the interior.

On reaching the Central Station, the next stage in his journey, Marlow was met with the disappointing news that the steamer he was to command had sunk, her bottom torn off as the manager had suddenly attempted to make for the Inner Station without waiting for him. Here Marlow also heard about Kurtz, though no longer with admiration but with resentment and fear. He set to work immediately to repair his boat but couldn't do much without rivets, which took two months to arrive from the Outer Station. Meanwhile a band of explorers, calling themselves 'the Eldorado Exploring Expedition' and headed by the manager's uncle, arrived at the Central Station. These did not even pretend to have come on a philanthropic mission; they talked unashamedly of the riches they could extract from the country. One night Marlow overheard a conversation between the manager and his uncle which gave him to understand that the manager was doing his best to delay relieving Kurtz, lying very ill at the Inner Station, in the hope that nature would remove this undesirable rival.

Three months after his arrival at the Central Station, Marlow at last left with the manager and a few 'pilgrims' for the Inner Station, which it took them another two months to reach. In all those months Marlow's curiosity about Kurtz had turned into a sense of growing expectation at the prospect of meeting this man who, in his rival's own words, was 'an emissary of pity, and science, and progress' (p. 40). On the way up-river Marlow keenly felt the power of attraction of the wilderness but was prevented from going ashore by the need to be attentive to his work.

With difficulty they reached the Inner Station, where they were welcomed by a young Russian dressed like a harlequin. While the manager and a few pilgrims went on shore, the harlequin came on board and confessed to Marlow his unbounded admiration for Kurtz's eloquence and ideas. He told Marlow in confidence that Kurtz had ordered an attack on the steamboat. Directing his field-glass towards Kurtz's house, Marlow realised that the knobs on the poles of the fence were actually dried human heads. It so horrified him that he refused to hear more from the harlequin about the rites and ceremonies staged by the natives in honour of Kurtz.

Meanwhile Kurtz was being carried on board, a very ill and emaciated man, a mere voice, as Marlow now insists, but still a deep, vibrating and eloquent one. He was followed to the shore by a crowd of natives. A magnificent woman, Kurtz's black mistress, appeared and raised her arms in a dramatic gesture that seemed to release swift shadows before she disappeared again. Shortly afterwards, the manager's unfavourable comments on Kurtz drove Marlow to side with the latter, glad to have at least a 'choice of nightmares' (p. 79). After midnight, when all were asleep on board, Marlow looked into the cabin where Kurtz had been lying and saw that he was not there. He did not betray him, but went on shore alone after him and managed to bring him back by outwitting him and breaking the spell that drew him to the wilderness. As they journeyed away from the 'heart of darkness', Kurtz discoursed eloquently about his ideas and his plans almost until the moment of his death, unaware of the discrepancy between his words and his actions. He gave Marlow a report he had written on the 'Suppression of Savage Customs', having forgotten all about his own postscript, 'Exterminate all the brutes!' (p. 66). Only at the very last instant did he seem to pass judgement on his life when he cried out 'The horror! The horror!' (p. 86).

Marlow himself nearly died of fever but came back to Brussels, the wiser for his experience and irritated by the ignorance and complacency of the people he met in the street. He was visited by several acquaintances and relatives of Kurtz, who each gave him a different picture of the 'great' man. He fulfilled what he saw as a last duty to Kurtz by visiting his Intended (his fiancée), about whom he had heard so much from Kurtz himself. As he entered the house towards evening his vision of Kurtz as a voracious shadow seemed to enter with him. The impressions of darkness and light that Marlow gathered from the drawing-room converged on the girl, for she was dressed in black and had a lofty forehead on which the light took refuge as the room grew darker. In the ensuing conversation Marlow was made uneasy once more, then desperate and even angry by the girl's

unquestioned admiration for Kurtz's greatness and eloquence and her deep
conviction that 'he died as he lived' (p. 94). He did not undeceive her,
however, nor take away the 'great and saving illusion' (p. 93) that sustained
her. When asked what Kurtz's last words were, he actually lied and said that
his last words had been her name.

Marlow's tale over, the first narrator concludes the narrative. The
Thames which, at the beginning of the novel, he saw flowing in 'tranquil
dignity' crowded with memories of the feats of British conquerors, he now
sees flowing 'sombre under an overcast sky … into the heart of an immense
darkness' (p. 95).

DETAILED SUMMARIES

Heart of Darkness consists of three fairly long chapters. It is possible,
however, to divide the narrative into a series of episodes which roughly
represent significant stages in Marlow's expedition. Naturally, this
division is not Joseph Conrad's but has been devised to help the student
in his close reading of the text. The full meaning of each episode can only
be assessed by keeping in mind the novel as a whole, for the narrative is
full of parallels, contrasts and echoes.

CHAPTER 1

EPISODE 1   **Description of the setting, the Thames estuary with its
contrasts of light and darkness. First narrator's thoughts
on British conquerors. Presentation of Marlow, the
second and major narrator. He begins his story. His
impressions of Brussels and of the Company's
headquarters**

From the beginning to 'I felt as though … I were about to set off for the centre of
the earth' (p. 27)

The novel opens with a description of the Thames Estuary at the end of the
day. The light over the estuary contrasts with the gloom over London, and
the five men on board the *Nellie* are in a silent, pensive mood. The first
narrator feels the 'spirit of the past' (p. 18) prevailing in their present

environment, and meditates on Britain's past conquerors and explorers – men who, starting from that same estuary, contributed to the wealth and fame of their country and sometimes carried the torch of civilisation to the ends of the earth. As if he could read his thoughts Marlow suddenly says: 'And this also … has been one of the dark places of the earth' (p. 19). He was not thinking of Britain's glorious past but of its dark ages when it was invaded by the Romans, who would have been fascinated by its wilderness. He insists that, whereas the Romans were mere robbers, contemporary colonisers are saved by efficiency and the 'idea' behind colonialism. After a short pause Marlow introduces his story as if it had no connection with colonial expeditions. He explains that he got his command of a steamer to travel up the Congo through the help of an aunt who knew a high official in the continental company that administered the Congo. He was appointed as the replacement of a Dane called Fresleven, speared in retaliation for killing an old village chief with whom he had quarrelled over two hens.

Marlow's first contact with the colonial enterprise begins in Brussels, the city that reminds him of a 'whited sepulchre' (p. 24). A dead silence prevails in the vicinity of the company headquarters. Marlow is briefly but ceremoniously interviewed in the 'sanctuary' (p. 25) of the company director. This troubles him, though not as much as the presence in the waiting room of two women, one fat and old, the other slim and younger, who are both knitting with black wool uninterruptedly. The company secretary, who has told Marlow he is not such a fool as to go to Africa himself, takes him to a doctor's for the necessary medical examination. The doctor measures Marlow's skull and to Marlow's question 'Are you an alienist?' he answers 'Every doctor should be – a little' (p. 26). When Marlow goes to say goodbye to his aunt, he realises that she is convinced he is taking the light of civilisation to 'ignorant millions' (p. 27). It makes him feel an impostor. He also has a queer feeling that he is about to travel to 'the centre of the earth' (p. 27).

> The first episode presents the development of the novel in a nutshell. As Marlow's story will show, the contrast between light and darkness in the setting conveys a duality also to be found in men and their enterprises. In traditional symbolism, light is normally associated with civilisation and its ideals, with enlightenment, consciousness and

self-knowledge; while darkness usually represents the wilderness, ignorance and evil. We may have the impression at first that Joseph Conrad subscribes to this conventional distinction – but he soon undermines it. Whereas the first narrator thinks of the heroic deeds of British conquerors (though he does mention that they were after gold and fame), Marlow sees the Roman invaders, the civilised men of 'very old times' (p. 20) facing a dark and hostile continent. But he also sees them as violent men robbing what they could from the invaded country. This already shows that the so-called bringers of light, who faced the darkness of the wilderness, were themselves agents of darkness. Although Marlow asserts that 'we' (which can refer to British colonists or contemporary colonisers in general) are different from the Romans, his definition of colonialism is universal and applies to all colonisers. It stresses the ambivalent nature of colonialism:

The conquest of the earth, which mostly means the taking it away from those
who have a different complexion or slightly flatter noses than ourselves, is
not a pretty thing when you look into it too much. What redeems it is the idea
only ... something you can set up, and bow down before, and offer a sacrifice to....
(p. 21)

Marlow's tale so far has several effects. It corrects the first narrator's simple optimism and unawareness by pointing to the evil of conquest and referring indirectly to the conquered people's view of the matter. It suggests that the colonial expedition, though a national enterprise, is also an ordeal testing individuals and revealing to them their susceptibility to being fascinated by the 'abomination' of the wilderness and of their own dark instincts. It also gives the reader a sense of the rise and fall of civilisations. The once powerful Roman Empire has disappeared while Britain, once a dark continent, has built an empire which may one day pass away too.

Marlow's view of Brussels as a 'whited sepulchre' with its connotation of hypocrisy and deadliness, the attitude and allusions of the people he meets there and his aunt's assumption that he is a gifted creature who goes to Africa as a kind of apostle; these sow in him the seed of an as yet undefinable malaise.

Finally, the first narrator makes an important comment on Marlow's narrative method, and at a further remove, Joseph Conrad's (p. 20). (See Narrative Technique.)

the flood had made the tide had risen

Sir Francis Drake (*c.*1543–96) one of the most famous Elizabethan seamen, who commanded the *Golden Hind* on a journey to South America, partly to make discoveries, partly for plunder

Sir John Franklin (1786–1847) an English admiral and explorer who commanded an expedition to the Northwest Passage on the *Erebus* and the *Terror*

mizzen-mast the mast aft of the main mast in a ship

Falernian wine from a district of Campania in Southern Italy. This wine was highly appreciated by the Romans

Ravenna a large Roman base in northern Italy

whited sepulchre a phrase used by Christ to denounce the hypocrisy of scribes and Pharisees (Matthew 23:27)

there was a vast amount of red red was the colour of British overseas possessions on the map

Ave! ... Morituri te salutant (Latin) Hail! ... those who are about to die salute you

Plato (428–348BC) a Greek philosopher

du calme, du calme (French) 'keep cool' or 'don't get excited'

adieu goodbye

EPISODE 2 **Along the African coast – Marlow's first impression of 'the merry dance of death and trade'. Description of 'the grove of death' where exhausted Africans are left to die while the white accountant keeps his books 'in apple-pie order'. Marlow's two-hundred-mile trek towards the Central station**

From 'I left in a French steamer' (p. 27) to 'He is waiting!' (p. 36)

Marlow travels to Africa on a French steamer. He is fascinated by the coast of the African continent which presents itself to him as an enigma, an impression enhanced by the sense of isolation he experiences among men with whom he has nothing in common. Only the noisy surf and an occasional boat paddled by sturdy negroes restore his sense of reality and make him feel he is in contact with something meaningful and real. Once they see a man-of-war firing insanely and incomprehensibly into an apparently empty continent, although someone assures Marlow they are firing at 'enemies'. After several stops at trading posts with farcical names, they reach the mouth of the Congo river and Marlow boards a steamer that will take him up-river to the company's Outer Station.

The captain of the boat, a young Swede, expresses his bitter contempt for the 'government chaps' and tells Marlow about a countryman of his who committed suicide shortly after reaching the Congo. When they arrive at the Outer Station, Marlow comes into contact for the first time with the reality of the colonial exploitation. The land itself is being devastated by repeated blastings, even of areas that are not in the way of the projected railway. Black slaves, chained to each other with an iron collar on their necks, carry baskets of earth from one place to another. When Marlow walks down to the river to keep out of their way, he comes upon a nightmarish scene: the ghostly figures of dying natives – overworked, starved and too weak to move – recline in the shade. Marlow feels he has 'stepped into the gloomy circle of some Inferno' (p. 31). 'Horror-struck' (p. 32), he climbs towards the station and meets a white man so elegantly and spotlessly dressed in white that Marlow takes him for a sort of vision. This is the chief accountant, whom Marlow sincerely admires and respects for what he has accomplished; the preservation of his impeccable appearance and the perfect keeping of his books in the midst of the surrounding confusion and the 'demoralisation of the land' (p. 33). The accountant, however, cannot stand the groans of a dying man left in his office to await a passage home, and when some natives in the yard are too noisy he comments that 'one comes to hate those savages – hate them to death' (p. 34).

After ten days Marlow starts on a two-hundred-mile trek towards the Central Station. Already at the Outer Station Marlow foresaw that in the Congo he would 'become acquainted with a flabby, pretending, weak-eyed devil of a rapacious and pitiless folly' (p. 31). Arriving at the Central Station after a trying journey, he sees immediately that this 'flabby devil' rules the place. He is told that the steamer he is to command has sunk and that the manager is expecting him.

It is clear from the beginning that Marlow's journey calls for several interpretations and that the narrative develops on at least two planes, the actual and the symbolic. Marlow's very concrete rendering of his journey also evokes an expedition into the psyche. To give but one example of the double meaning of the narrative, when Marlow steps 'into the gloomy circle of some inferno' at the Outer Station, the disturbing shadows he comes upon are exploited men, but they also evoke those who suffer in Hell, as usually represented in Christian iconography, and, as we shall see, they can be seen as symbolic of so many inner selves.

The expedition is a personal ordeal for Marlow, and his reactions to what he discovers are an essential part of the narrative. His first impression is that the white man is an intruder in Africa. He violates the country, while trade (mainly a scramble for ivory) only brings despair and death in its wake. The first negroes Marlow sees on the edge of the continent are full of vitality, but as he goes inland, he meets first men reduced to slavery, then mere shadows left to die like animals. The darkness of the 'inferno' at the Outer Station is the reality the whites have brought with them, and the light of civilisation subsists only in appearances: for example in the light attire of the accountant and his devotion to apparent order (his impeccable accounts which nevertheless represent real money interests) rather than the values of civilisation. The whites' work in Africa, moreover, appears to be utterly useless or inefficient. Marlow's matter-of-fact tone enhances the impression of horror created by his words. It also adds to the irony which pervades his narrative and arises from the discrepancy between the apparent commonplaceness of some of his statements and the reality they convey. When, for example, he comes across a vast artificial hole and wonders why it has been dug, he declares 'It might have been connected with the philanthropic desire of giving the criminals something to do' (p. 31). The juxtaposition of 'philanthropic desire' with 'criminals' expresses indirectly but forcefully the monstrosity of the whites' enterprise.

railway-truck when Joseph Conrad went to the Congo, a railway was being built from Matadi to Kinshassa in order to by-pass the thirty-two rapids in the lower Congo, which made navigation extremely difficult

raw-matter it is the natives whom Marlow calls 'raw-matter' because of the way in which they are being treated. During the slave trade Africans were called 'stock', an expression which dehumanised them and justified their being treated like animals

Inferno a place of torment and suffering that suggests Hell. Also the title of one of the books in the *Divina commedia* (1310–21), the great Christian poem written by the Italian poet Dante Alighieri (1265–1321)

a bit of white worsted a piece of white fabric made of worsted yarns

a propitiatory act an act intended to appease or conciliate a higher authority or power

a first-class agent this does not mean an excellent agent – although the accountant would clearly consider it fitting to apply this epithet to Kurtz – but one of higher rank

EPISODE 3   **At the Central Station Marlow meets successively the Manager, a Brickmaker and the El Dorado Exploring Expedition led by the Manager's uncle. The boat he is to command has been sunk and he is made to wait for weeks to get rivets to repair it. Marlow hears more about Kurtz**

From 'I did not see the real significance' (p. 36) to the end of Chapter 1 (p. 46)

Immediately after his arrival at the Central Station, Marlow is received by the manager who does not even invite him to sit down after his twenty-mile walk in the jungle that day. The manager inspires uneasiness, not because of his superiority, but because (as Marlow soon discovers) 'there was nothing within him' and he was once heard to say '"Men who come out here should have no entrails"' (p. 37). This seems to be the case with the brickmaker, a first-class agent supposed to be making bricks, although none are to be seen around the station. Marlow suspects that if he poked his forefinger through him he 'would find nothing inside but a little loose dirt, maybe' (p. 41). The other white men at the station seem equally aimless, their only concern being for ivory, a word ringing constantly in the air. Because they seem to be praying to it, turning it into a god, and carry long staves as if to help them on a pilgrimage, Marlow calls them 'faithless pilgrims' (p. 38).

On the day after his arrival Marlow sets down to work and repair his boat, but he cannot do so for lack of rivets. He knows there are plenty of them at the Outer Station and that a messenger travels there from the Central Station every week, but he will have to wait about two months before he gets any. He is surprised that the manager proved to be right in his prediction that the steamer would take three months to repair. Meanwhile a fire breaks out at the Central Station, and an obviously innocent African is cruelly beaten up for it. While others ineffectually try to stop the fire (one pilgrim even carries a pail with a hole in its bottom), Marlow starts a conversation with the brickmaker, who invites him to his hut. He soon realises, however, that the brickmaker is trying to pump him about his acquaintances in Brussels. When the brickmaker gets angry at Marlow's failure to respond, the latter gets up and only then notices a small painting done by Kurtz 'representing a woman, draped and blindfolded, carrying a lighted torch' (p. 40).

Marlow, who has already been struck by the manager's reference to Kurtz during their first conversation, asks the brickmaker outright who this Mr Kurtz is. He receives an ambivalent answer, being told in a dutiful yet sceptical tone that Kurtz is 'an emissary of pity, and science, and progress' (p. 40), the kind of man who is needed to serve the civilising cause of Europe. Kurtz is a representative of the new 'gang of virtue' and the people who sent him are the same who recommended Marlow. The latter now understands why he is looked upon with suspicion by the jealous manager and pilgrims. He nevertheless asks the brickmaker to help him to get rivets and, back on his boat, dances like a lunatic at the thought of getting them. The rivets, however, do not come so soon. Instead, the Eldorado Exploring Expedition, a 'gang' of greedy exploiters led by the manager's uncle, comes to the station.

In this section Marlow introduces two *leitmotives* of his narrative. One is that 'out there there were no external checks' (p. 37) on one's behaviour. The other is that work alone can help one keep a hold 'on the redeeming facts of life' (p. 38). This becomes particularly important in the other two chapters when Marlow, like Kurtz, is tempted to give in to the wilderness. At this stage it is clear that the main source of temptation for the white man is ivory and that the pilgrims, who have deified it, are prepared to go to any length to get some. Marlow is not tempted by ivory but he is greatly impressed by the silent powerfulness of the primeval forest which, like the African coast before, presents itself as an enigma to him. The forest is where ivory is to be found and the place where Kurtz lives. Although Marlow does not know yet what he will find in the heart of darkness, a link is unobtrusively suggested between men's lust for ivory and the forest as a place where they are tempted to yield to their lower instincts. Marlow can therefore ask 'Could we handle that dumb thing, or would it handle us?' (p. 42). This question anticipates the more specific one he later asks about Kurtz: 'Everything belonged to him ... The thing was to know what he belonged to' (p. 65). So far, however, what Marlow has heard about Kurtz from the accountant, the manager and the brickmaker has merely made him curious about him. Indeed, all he has seen of the white man's behaviour in Africa represents one kind of evil or another: lunatic or futile action, inefficiency, ruthless exploitation of the natives and, at the Central Station, hollowness and pretence. What is Kurtz really like, who is presented as an idealist even by those who fear him?

Jack an ill-mannered fellow

assegais slender hardwood spears

there is something ... in the world allowing one man to steal a horse while another must not look at a halter a certain way of coveting a halter is far worse than stealing the horse itself

papier-mâché Mephistopheles an unreal, unsubstantial devil

Huntley and Palmers a well-known biscuit making company

ichthyosaurus a prehistoric reptile

El Dorado a fabulously wealthy city or country that sixteenth-century explorers thought existed in South America. It justified the conquest of the New World and the extermination of natives

CHAPTER 2

EPISODE 1   **Marlow overhears a conversation between the manager and his uncle to the effect that they hope 'nature' will have the better of Kurtz, a dangerous competitor. At last, the boat repaired, Marlow begins his journey towards Kurtz. His impressions of the forest and of the men he and his companions occasionally see on the river banks**

From 'One evening as I was lying flat on the deck of my steamboat' (p. 46) to 'beyond my power of meddling' (p. 54)

One evening Marlow overhears a conversation between the manager and his uncle. They are talking about Kurtz and both hope that the jungle, which kills off so many people, will also remove him from the manager's way to success.

At last Marlow's steamboat is repaired and he leaves with the manager and a few pilgrims. As he progresses from the Central to the Inner Station, Marlow feels as if he were 'travelling back to the earliest beginnings of the world' (p. 49). He is now penetrating the unknown territory of the wilderness, and the philosophic comments the journey elicits from him remind us that it is also a metaphor for an inner exploration.

As he comes into contact with a world untrammelled by the trappings of civilisation, Marlow's first overwhelming impression is that an inner truth is hidden in both nature and men. He senses the truth of nature in its potent and mysterious 'stillness' (p. 49) even though the earth is here 'a thing monstrous and free' (p. 51). The enthusiastic outbreak of the 'prehistoric' men on the shore as they watch the passing steamboat is unadulterated reaction: 'Joy, fear, sorrow, devotion, valour, rage', what Marlow calls 'truth stripped of its cloak of time' (p. 52). He asserts that in order to face that truth man needs 'inborn strength' and a 'deliberate belief' which he opposes to mere principles. These, to him, are like 'rags that would fly off at the first good shake' (p. 52). Marlow's own deliberate belief seems to be in the efficiency of work, which helps him resist the appeal of the wilderness. We are here reminded of his earlier assertion: 'I like what is in the work – the chance to find yourself. Your own reality' (p. 44).

This capacity to assert oneself through work is what Marlow means when he says 'I have a voice, too' (p. 52). He soon finds support for his belief when he discovers an abandoned hut on the shore. A white man has left there a pile of wood for Marlow's steamboat and a message 'approach cautiously'. This can only refer to the Inner Station. Near the entrance of the hut Marlow finds a book called *An Inquiry into some Points of Seamanship* by an old naval man, and recognises in it 'a singleness of intention, an honest concern for the right way of going to work' (p. 53). This section ends with Marlow's conjectures about his forthcoming meeting with Kurtz. He now feels that his penetration into the heart of darkness is exclusively a progress towards Kurtz.

> The assertion by the manager's uncle that 'Anything – anything can be done in this country' (p. 48), an illustration of Marlow's conviction that 'out there there were no external checks', as well as the uncle's appeal 'to the lurking death, to the hidden evil, to the profound darkness of its [the land's] heart' (p. 48) show that evil in nature is brought out by people and reflects the evil in their own hearts. It would be a mistake and a simplification to consider the heart of darkness itself as a metaphor for evil. Its effect in this passage is to make Marlow think about humankind in general and the respective meanings of white and black cultures.

> Humankind, particularly the white man with his technological achievement, is still very small compared to grandiose nature – for example, 'the little begrimed steamboat' crawling 'like a sluggish beetle' between 'the high walls' (pp. 50–1) of the jungle. Moreover, just as the white man must be in the natives' eyes 'an insoluble mystery from the sea' (p. 30), so the black man is an enigma for the white explorer: 'The prehistoric man was cursing us, praying to us, welcoming us – who could tell? We were cut off from the comprehension of our surroundings' (p. 51). In effect Marlow is discovering that one type of 'man' is not superior to another, but that each is a mystery for the other. The white man, however, can understand what he shares with prehistoric man if he is prepared to face humanity's past in himself: 'The mind of man is capable of anything – because everything is in it, all the past as well as all the future' (p. 52). People can face what they discover in the prehistoric world with what Marlow calls 'inborn strength' and 'deliberate belief' (p. 52), which clearly imply faithfulness to what one is and awareness

of one's capacities i.e. 'authenticity'. The fireman, like Marlow, is prevented from going ashore 'for a howl and a dance' (p. 52) and he is forced to do work unnatural to him which he does not understand. People (whether white or black) faced with the incomprehensible and lacking 'inborn strength' are less capable of restraint in a situation of strain than the 'cannibals', 'Fine fellows ... men one could work with' (p. 50).

tight-rope a rope stretched taut on which acrobats perform
half-a-crown a tumble the price an acrobat gets for each acrobatic feat. Half-a-crown was worth two shillings and sixpence, one-eighth of the pound sterling, before decimal currency was introduced

EPISODE 2 **As the steamboat approaches the Inner Station, it is attacked by natives whose cries seem to express despair rather than aggressiveness. Both white and black men seem equally capable of restraint (Marlow and the 'cannibals') or of cowardice (the other white men and the African helmsman)**

From 'Towards the evening of the second day' (p. 54) to 'Here, give me some tobacco.' ... (p. 63)

The manager again delays their approach to the Inner Station but this time Marlow must admit that to proceed in the dark would be dangerous. Marlow describes the atmosphere prevailing on the river in the vicinity of the Inner Station. The bush seems to be frozen into an unnatural state of trance, which makes men suspect that they are deaf as well as blind when night falls. In the morning a thick fog, at once 'blind' (p. 58) and 'more blinding than the night' (p. 55) envelops the whole area, and Marlow finds it extremely difficult to progress on the narrow reach of the river obstructed with dangerous snags. A very loud cry, to Marlow an expression of extreme and unrestrained grief, pierces the fog. He compares the reaction of the whites to this suddenly-revealed presence of natives on the shore with that of the cannibals on board. The whites are very nervous. On the contrary the blacks, who are also strangers in this area and as unfamiliar with it as the whites, remain calm and self-controlled although they ask Marlow to catch their hidden opponents for them to eat.

This reminds Marlow that the natives on the boat have not received any food for weeks. They have been forced to throw overboard the rotten hippo-meat that was their sole provision for the journey, and receive three pieces of brass wire every week to buy food which is not to be had anyway. Marlow meditates on the enigmatic source of the cannibals' self-restraint and 'inborn strength', for he is convinced that there is no more exasperating and ferocious torment than hunger. By contrast, the only restraint the manager is capable of is hypocrisy for he now declares 'I would be desolated if anything should happen to Mr. Kurtz before we came up' (p. 58).

Contrary to Marlow's assertion that they would not do so, the natives on shore attack the boat, although Marlow considers their action as a protective one, an attempt at repulse on the part of desperate men. The incomers are shot at with arrows which, to Marlow, seem harmless. The pilgrims, however, lose their self-control and blindly unload their Winchesters on to the bush. So does the black helmsman (spoiled by so-called civilisation, like the fireman). He opens the shutter of the pilot house (previously closed by Marlow) and fires. He is speared and dies with a familiar, then a questioning, glance at Marlow. The latter quickly pulls the boat's steam-whistle. The attack is checked instantly and another wail of despair arises from the bush. While Marlow anxiously changes his shoes, which are full of the helmsman's blood, he experiences a keen disappointment at the thought that Kurtz might also be dead. He realises that he thinks of Kurtz as 'a voice' (p. 63) and that he has been looking forward to a talk with Kurtz throughout the journey. He also realises that his sorrow at possibly missing that talk is as extravagant as the natives' cry of despair.

> In this passage the travellers on the steamboat are further isolated from anything they know. The reaction of black and white men to their disturbing position is clearly not a question of race, since both the pilgrims and the uprooted helmsman are incapable of restraint. Marlow is efficient and shows great presence of mind in keeping the boat clear of snags and pulling the steam-whistle which frightens their assailants. The manager (who has done his best to delay their arrival at the Inner Station, first by sinking the steamboat, then by not letting Marlow have rivets to repair it) is sincere when he says he would be sorry if Kurtz died before they came, because he wants to

keep up appearances. Towards both the natives and Kurtz he is determined to keep up what Marlow called earlier the 'sentimental' (p. 21) or 'philanthropic pretence' (p. 39) but there is no end to which he will not go to ensure his power over the colony in competition with Kurtz. By emphasising this point in a passage which, by comparison, shows the admirable restraint of the starving cannibals, Marlow suggests that the whites are guilty of an uncontrolled and devouring appetite for material riches (ivory) which is cannibalistic in nature. We shall see that an extreme form of it is to be found in Kurtz. The self-restraint of the cannibals remains a mystery to Marlow. But he notices that the helmsman, who, like the white man in Africa, has lost the support of his community by doing an incomprehensible job for the whites, dies utterly bewildered. The as yet unexplained grief of the natives on shore, and Marlow's own grief at the thought that he might be too late to hear Kurtz, are a significant comment on this man's power of eloquence. Marlow increases his listeners' (and the reader's) suspense about Kurtz by presenting it as an ambivalent gift: 'the gift of expression, the bewildering, the illuminating, the most exalted and the most contemptible, the pulsating stream of light, or the deceitful flow from the heart of an impenetrable darkness' (p. 63).

Martini-Henry a type of rifle
Winchester also a type of rifle, named after the manufacturer

EPISODE 3   **In a jump forward to a later part of his story, Marlow comments on his meeting with Kurtz, on the effect of Kurtz's eloquence and on the ambivalence of Kurtz's report. At the Inner Station, they are met by the 'harlequin' who expresses his great admiration for Kurtz**

From 'There was a pause of profound stillness' (p. 63) to the end of Chapter 2 (p. 71)

A deep sigh from one of his listeners stops Marlow in his narrative. The interruption makes him aware of his listeners' possible perplexity in reaction to his upsetting tale. After a short pause he launches into a fairly long digression (from p. 64 to p. 67). Its main import is a comparison between the situation of the white man in his own society and that of Kurtz in the jungle. In his own environment the white man is protected from his own worst instincts by the butcher, who satisfies his appetite, and the policeman, who keeps alive his fear of scandal, of the gallows and of the lunatic asylum. When he is deprived of these supports in the 'utter solitude' (p. 65) of the jungle, man must fall back upon his 'own innate strength' and his 'capacity for faithfulness' (p. 65) (another expression for 'deliberate belief' – p. 52).

Anticipating his meeting with Kurtz and the impression the latter made on him, Marlow asserts that in the solitude of the jungle Kurtz has been consumed by the wilderness outside and within himself. 'He had taken a high seat amongst the devils of the land' (p. 65) and was incapable of restraining his lust for possession. Marlow adds that all Europe had contributed to the making of Kurtz and that he had been asked by the International Society for the Suppression of Savage Customs to write a report for its guidance. Marlow has read the report, which was obviously written before Kurtz himself began to preside over 'unspeakable rites' (p. 66) offered to him. The report ominously started with the assertion that whites must necessarily appear to savages as supernatural beings. Yet Marlow confesses that he was greatly impressed by the report and Kurtz's 'burning noble words'; until he reached the postscript, clearly written much later, which read 'Exterminate all the brutes' (p. 66). Reflecting on this inner contradiction, Marlow concludes that Kurtz was not worth the helmsman's life lost for him.

This allusion to his helmsman who, Marlow comments, lacked restraint 'just like Kurtz' (p. 67), brings him back to the main strand of his narrative. He shocks the pilgrims by promptly throwing the helmsman's body overboard before his cannibal woodcutters are tempted by him. Shortly afterwards they reach the Inner Station and Marlow notices carved balls ornamenting posts around the house. They are welcomed by a funny white man dressed all in patches, who reminds Marlow of a harlequin. He has a boyish face 'overcast one moment and bright the next' (p. 69) and is a Russian. He calls the natives 'simple people' and confirms that it was the steam-whistle that frightened them. He expresses the greatest admiration for Kurtz, though from the first he appears to hide something from Marlow. But he keeps repeating that Kurtz 'has enlarged my [his] mind' (p. 70).

The effect of Marlow's long digression and of the contrast he draws between the white man's living conditions in Europe and in Africa is to warn the reader that, placed in similar circumstances, any white man might react like Kurtz. Marlow reflects Joseph Conrad's pessimism when he suggests that it is not the white man's conscience but his fear of the policeman and of public opinion that keeps him on the straight path. Moreover, it would seem that the 'innate strength' and 'faithfulness' which Marlow so much praises as means of resisting the wilderness only really help man to ignore it, to dig 'unostentatious holes' in which to bury 'dead hippo' (p. 65) – a metaphor both for the wilderness and for humanity's uncontrollable impulses.

This passage makes clear both Kurtz's dualism and Marlow's own ambivalent reaction to him. Kurtz sees himself as great ('Everything belonged to him' – p. 65) but he has in fact been reduced to a mere 'shade', an 'initiated wraith' (pp. 65–6). The natives have made a god of him and he looks upon himself in that light too. But the postscript to his report reveals that he is a bloodthirsty brute. His conviction of being a superior being and his insatiable hunger for power have led him to behave like a god and to arrogate to himself the right to destroy all those who are different from himself. That all Europe should have contributed to his making indicates that he represents the greed and will-to-power of all European states. Marlow's feeling for him is a mixture of admiration for his 'unbounded power of eloquence' (p. 66) and of utter contempt. The harlequin's alternating smiles and frowns and his uneasiness present Marlow with another mystery.

harlequin a quick-witted servant who is a stock character in the *commedia dell'arte*; he usually wears a mask and parti-coloured tights

CHAPTER 3

EPISODE 1   **Marlow's conversation with the harlequin reveals Kurtz's insatiable and uncontrolled thirst for ivory. Marlow realises that the balls on stakes around Kurtz's house are dried human heads. Kurtz's black mistress appears, gorgeous and tragic but wild**

From 'I looked at him, lost in astonishment' (p. 71) to 'Ah, well, it's all over now' (p. 78)

Marlow admires the harlequin's resilience and his unreflecting audacity. He envies his glamour and pure spirit of adventure but not his thoughtless admiration of Kurtz. Though the harlequin is reluctant to tell the whole truth, Marlow gradually makes out that after he had no more goods to trade with, Kurtz raided the country for ivory with the help of an inland tribe who had become his unconditional followers and 'adored' him. In spite of the harlequin's entreaty Kurtz had refused to leave the Inner Station while there was still time. The harlequin had nursed him through two illnesses, yet Kurtz had threatened to kill him if he did not relinquish to him (Kurtz) what little ivory he had. This the harlequin found quite justifiable. While they are talking Marlow has taken his binoculars, and looking at the carved balls ornamenting the fence around Kurtz's house, he suddenly realises they are not ornaments but dried human heads on stakes. To Marlow these show that Kurtz 'lacked restraint in the gratification of his various lusts' (p. 74) and also that he was 'hollow at the core' (p. 74). Again, he anticipates what is to come by suggesting that the knowledge of his deficiency came to Kurtz at the very last. Meanwhile, he refuses to hear more of Kurtz's relations with the natives (what he has termed 'unspeakable rites' – p. 66) and cannot hide his stupefaction from the harlequin, who asserts that the heads on the stakes are those of 'rebels'. The harlequin declares that he himself is a simple man and does not understand the complex temptations to which a great man like Kurtz is apparently liable.

At this juncture, Kurtz himself appears carried on a stretcher. Marlow sees him as a 'phantom' and a 'shadow', an 'animated image of death' with a 'weirdly voracious aspect' (p. 76). His voice, however, is still impressive and he manages to restrain the natives who have uttered a shrill cry at his departure and come out of the bush. Kurtz is laid down in one the boat's small cabins, and the manager joins him while Marlow and the Russian look at the shore. A magnificent black woman, whom Marlow describes in some detail, now makes her appearance. She is at once savage and superb. Before disappearing again she throws her arms up in a dramatic gesture and at the same time swift shadows gather around the river and the boat which until then were in the sunshine. The harlequin expresses his hostility towards her. It seems that she dislikes him too and once quarrelled with Kurtz about him but, again, the harlequin can only repeat: 'I don't understand' (p. 78).

The harlequin prepares Marlow for his meeting with Kurtz. He, too, is an ambivalent character; his youthfulness and extraordinary capacity to survive, together with the efficiency it implies, contrast with his indiscriminate adoration of Kurtz, for he cannot say precisely in what way Kurtz has enriched his life. There is an ironic contrast between his reiterated statements: '[Kurtz] has enlarged my mind' and 'I don't understand'. This reflects as much on the nature of Kurtz's eloquence (beautiful but vague, as Marlow's own judgement shows) as on the harlequin.

Marlow first meets Kurtz just after becoming aware that the ornaments on stakes around his house are human heads and he has commented on Kurtz's hollowness. This seems to contradict an earlier suggestion that, unlike the pilgrims, Kurtz is not hollow because he has at least ideals that can become corrupted. He clearly does not belong to the category of man of whom Marlow said: 'I take it, no fool ever made a bargain for his soul with the devil: the fool is too much of a fool, or the devil too much of a devil' (p. 65). Kurtz, however, is hollow in that he lacks the moral capacity to resist the wilderness. He has no moral sense on which to act and is not even aware of the discrepancy between his very real idealism and his actions.

The superb black woman who appears on the shore is clearly an embodiment of the wilderness, but again, we must beware of attributing too simple.a symbolism to Marlow's narrative. The tragic sorrow on her face suggests grief rather than evil. Moreover, her effect on Marlow now and at the moment of departure is ambivalent. He is at once repelled by her and full of admiration.

Jupiter   the chief god in Roman mythology

EPISODE 2   **The harlequin tells Marlow that it was Kurtz who ordered the attack of the steamboat. After midnight Marlow realises that Kurtz has gone on shore alone. Marlow follows him, struggles with him and manages to bring him back onto the boat**

From 'At this moment I heard Kurtz's deep voice' (p. 78) to 'I could see nothing more for smoke' (p. 84)

Marlow's conversation with the harlequin is interrupted by Kurtz's loud protest, behind the curtain of the cabin, that the manager has not come to save him but the ivory; and that in fact it was Kurtz who had to save the manager and his companions from being attacked by Kurtz's resentful native followers. When the manager comes out of the cabin he complains that Kurtz's method is unsound and that the trade will suffer. Marlow's first rejoinder is that Kurtz has 'no method at all' (p. 78) but he checks the manager's exultation at this by asserting that Kurtz is a remarkable man. He is therefore lumped with Kurtz as unsound but finds it a relief from the manager's vile hypocrisy and is glad to have at least 'a choice of nightmares' (p. 79). Before leaving the steamboat the harlequin reveals to Marlow that it was Kurtz who ordered the natives to attack it. Because he is concerned about Kurtz's reputation, he warns Marlow against what Kurtz might yet do.

Marlow wakes up shortly after midnight and recalls the harlequin's warning. He perceives that deep within the forest black columnar shapes move around the red gleams of a fire. Marlow is aroused from his half-awakened state by the sudden yells of the natives. Looking into Kurtz's cabin, he realises that it is empty. His reaction is one of 'pure abstract terror' due to the 'moral shock' he has received as if he were confronted with something 'monstrous' (p. 81). Marlow, however, does not betray Kurtz. He goes ashore after him recalling (rather irrelevantly, it seems) the old knitting woman in Brussels, and imagining he might be left alone in the jungle. He overtakes Kurtz with whom he fights as with a 'Shadow' (p. 82), being aware all the time that if Kurtz chose to make a row they would all be lost. He appeals to Kurtz's pride in what he has achieved in order to break the spell of the wilderness on him, and persuades him to return to the boat. Recalling this episode Marlow is prompted to another short digression, first about the terrible isolation of Kurtz's soul which 'had looked within itself, and … had gone mad' (p. 83), then, anticipating again, about the significance of Kurtz's last words. When Kurtz is at last back in his cabin Marlow feels as if he had been carrying half a ton, although the emaciated Kurtz is hardly heavier than a child.

The next day, as they are about to leave, the shore fills with frantic natives whose deep murmurs are like 'some satanic litany' (p. 84). Kurtz's black mistress is there again. She puts out her arms and shouts something after the boat which is taken up by the crowd. To Marlow's question, 'Do you understand this?' (p. 84), Kurtz answers with a smile of indefinable meaning, 'Do I not?' (p. 84). As they leave, Marlow blows the steam-whistle and disperses the natives. Only the superb black woman does not flinch and remains with her arms tragically stretched out after the boat.

> Another expression of Joseph Conrad's pessimism is to be found in Marlow's assertion that he has 'a choice of nightmares' (p. 79) – a choice, that is, between the vile hypocrisy of the manager and the corruption of Kurtz. Marlow's knowledge that Kurtz has ordered the attack on the boat, together with the moral shock he receives when he realises that Kurtz has gone ashore, confirm (if need be) Kurtz's total surrender to his baser instincts. That Marlow should be shocked morally and not just afraid of the very real danger in which they all are emphasises the nature of his quest. It is not just an errand to retrieve Kurtz. His soul is at stake and so is Marlow's. His appeal to Kurtz's pride and egoism also confirms the source of Kurtz's corruption; it is essentially the result of his boundless will-to-power. Yet Marlow does not betray him then or later. Once more he creates suspense, first about the reason of his fidelity to Kurtz, then about Kurtz's last words. By insisting that he does not understand his own behaviour, he stimulates his listeners (and the readers) to reflect on it. Kurtz's assertion that he understands the appeal of the natives and of his black mistress contrasts with the simplicity and bewilderment of the harlequin.

EPISODE 3   **Kurtz's pronouncement 'The horror! The horror!' followed by his death. The boy announces 'Mistah Kurtz – he dead'. Marlow's own illness. His return to Brussels. His lie to Kurtz's Intended**

From 'The brown current ran swiftly' (p. 85) to the end

The boat now travels down-river towards the sea much faster than it did upwards. The pilgrims still look upon Marlow as an associate of Kurtz and this is to some extent justified by the fact that Kurtz talks to Marlow alone, making him the confidant of his great hopes but confirming at the same time the discrepancy between these and the 'hollow sham' (p. 85) he has become. His life is fast running out, and it seems that almost to the end he remains self-deceived. However, just before he dies, it is 'as though a veil had been rent' (p. 86) and Marlow reads on his face contradictory emotions of pride and ruthless power on one hand, terror and hopeless despair on the other. Kurtz's last moment is one of 'complete knowledge', and he exclaims 'The horror! The horror!' (p. 86). This Marlow interprets as 'a judgment upon the adventures of his soul on this earth' (p. 87). Shortly afterwards the manager's boy announces in the now famous words: 'Mistah Kurtz – he dead' (p. 87).

Marlow, too, nearly died. But, he says, 'I remained to dream the nightmare out to the end, and to show my loyalty to Kurtz once more' (p. 87). He describes his unexciting contest with death. He has merely peeped over the edge of the precipice and now wonders whether, had he really died, he would have been able to utter as eloquent a cry as Kurtz. This, to him, is 'an affirmation, a moral victory' (p. 88) dearly paid for. When Marlow returned to the 'sepulchral city' (Brussels) he could hardly bear the complacency of its inhabitants. He now realises, however, that his impressions were subjective, that after his experience in the jungle he was not in a normal state of mind and that it was his 'imagination that wanted soothing' (p. 88). He receives the visit of several people who have known Kurtz and who each emphasise a different aspect of his personality. The complete picture this creates gives indeed the impression that Kurtz was a 'universal genius' (p. 89). To each visitor, except the threatening official, Marlow gives some of Kurtz's writings. Finally, Marlow is stimulated to visit Kurtz's Intended after looking at her picture and noticing 'the delicate shade of truthfulness upon those [her] features' (p. 90). As he enters the house Marlow has a vision of Kurtz opening his mouth voraciously and feels as if the wilderness were entering with him. When the girl appears in the room it is getting darker and all the light seems to gather on her pure brow. Marlow is aware of the depth of her sorrow; he realises she is not likely to be the plaything of time, and he suddenly sees her and Kurtz together. In the ensuing conversation she questions Marlow eagerly about Kurtz, or rather she asks him questions and suggests answers to them herself, anxious to hear Marlow confirm that she knew and understood Kurtz best, loved him best, and that Kurtz was a great and noble man. All this time the darkness increases in the room and contrasts with the light on her head. Marlow does not contradict the Intended; he tells her what she wants to hear in spite of his anger and despair, of which she is utterly unaware. At one stage she puts out her arms in exactly the same way as Kurtz's black mistress. Then she wants to know how Kurtz died and what his last words were. Marlow does not betray Kurtz. He lies and tells her that the last word Kurtz pronounced was her name. He has the impression that the house might collapse but, he says, 'the heavens do not fall for such a trifle' (p. 94). His excuse for lying is that 'It would have been too dark – too dark altogether' (p. 94).

Marlow's tale is now ended. The first narrator once more comments on his Buddha-like position and closes the narrative by saying that 'the tranquil waterway ... seemed to lead into the heart of an immense darkness' (p. 95).

> Marlow's renewed assertion that Kurtz is only a voice emphasises once more the nature of Kurtz's power, which lies wholly in the seductiveness of his eloquence; it also stresses his duality, the contrast between his idealism and the fake character of his achievement. Kurtz's insistence that one must always act for the right motives reveals the extent of his deception. It is worth comparing briefly Kurtz's last moment with the helmsman's. The latter gave Marlow a look 'like a claim of distant kinship affirmed' (p. 67), which suggests that the significance of his death may be relevant to all. The 'supreme moment' of his death becomes in Kurtz's case 'that supreme moment of complete knowledge' (p. 86). Kurtz can understand more clearly than the helmsman what is happening to him and that, too, is relevant to all for 'his stare ... was wide enough to embrace the whole universe, piercing enough to penetrate all the hearts that beat in the darkness' (p. 87). Whatever the truth Kurtz has glimpsed, Marlow sees its perception as a 'moral victory'. In other words, he approves of Kurtz's achievement of consciousness; that is why he keeps thinking of him as a remarkable man and remains loyal to him.

> When Marlow is back in Brussels the reader has the impression that he has escaped one kind of death but faces another, the death of the spirit. Indeed what strikes him is the blindness and 'folly' of the people he meets 'in the face of a danger it is [they are] unable to comprend' (p. 88). Apart from the official who visits Marlow, the others' praise of Kurtz emphasises once more the greatness of which he seems to have been truly capable. But without realising it, the

journalist puts his finger on the very danger of Kurtz's gifts when he says he ought to have gone into politics because he could electrify large meetings, could get himself to believe anything, and was an extremist. He thus puts into a nutshell all the reasons why Kurtz (and the European powers he clearly represents in this passage) could work up in himself and others a great enthusiasm for a cause which led him to the worst aberrations. This is brought home to the reader with greater force when Marlow visits the Intended and cannot dissociate his memory of the wilderness and of the voracious Kurtz from the idealism and the light that are so clearly impressed on her personality. Yet she too is self-deceived since she only wants from Marlow a confirmation of her faith in Kurtz. Marlow refuses to make her aware of the darkness in order to preserve her 'great and saving illusion' (p. 93). This brings to mind two other statements by Marlow. One is to the effect that the 'idea' behind the colonial enterprise redeems it (p. 21). The other is his assertion that women should stay in a 'beautiful world of their own' (p. 64).

Notice also the contrast between the first narrator's early description of the Thames as 'a waterway leading to the uttermost ends of the earth' (p. 18), and its leading 'into the heart of an immense darkness' (p. 95) at the end.

PART THREE

CRITICAL APPROACHES

CHARACTERISATION

Apart from Kurtz, Marlow, and his predecessor, Fresleven, none of the other characters are given a name. They are called after their function, which suggests that they are types rather than strongly individualised figures, and emphasises the symbolic meaning of Marlow's tale.

Critics disagree as to whether Marlow or Kurtz is the major character. It can be argued that they are equally important in so far as each is subjected to the same kind of experience in the African interior, though Kurtz obviously with a different purpose and for a much longer time than Marlow. The latter, however, recreates Joseph Conrad's own experience, evokes that of Kurtz and his personal reactions to it, while also showing in what way his journey to the Congo and his meeting with Kurtz affected him. Moreover, the way in which he tells his story (its narrative technique) is part of the meaning of the text.

MARLOW

In his introduction to *Youth*, the story in which Marlow appears for the first time as second, and chief, narrator, Joseph Conrad says of him: 'He haunts my hours of solitude, when, in silence, we lay our heads together in great comfort and harmony'. This might lead us to suppose that Marlow is Conrad's *alter ego* and a mere mouthpiece for him. It is not quite so, however. By using Marlow as an intermediary between himself and the other characters, Conrad achieves a detachment which it might have been more difficult for him to maintain had he dealt straightforwardly with autobiographical material. As it is, Marlow is at once involved in the story and his own progress in understanding is a major aspect of his narrative; he is also a commentator who, in spite of his numerous questions and his often non-committal tone, subtly directs the reader's response to his tale. His repeated self-questioning indirectly invites the reader to ask himself similar questions and inclines him/her to trust Marlow as a narrator, though not all readers do so. This usually depends on whether or not the reader identifies Marlow with Joseph Conrad. Unlike the third-person omniscient narrator of earlier fiction, Marlow does not attempt to impose his point of view authoritatively, though this is sometimes challenged by certain critics (see Critical History). We judge Marlow as a fallible human being with a normal capacity for good and evil and liable to make the same errors as those he denounces in others.

Much of the novel's significance grows out of Marlow's expedition and his return as a changed man. In one way at least he is an exceptional man: 'The worst that could be said of him was that he did not represent his class. He was a seaman, but he was a wanderer too, while most seamen lead, if one may so express it, a sedentary life. Their minds are of the stay-at-home order' (p. 19). This suggests that, unlike other sailors, Marlow has an active imaginative life and is a traveller in the 'country of the mind'. His comments on the 'pilgrims' and the way in which he dissociates himself from them shows that he is not self-interested as they are and that he has already progressed in self-knowledge. The same can be said of his encounters with the harlequin and Kurtz, which force him to define his own position. What differentiates him most from the other characters is his capacity for moral discrimination. Nevertheless, Marlow himself offers a good example of the complexity of human behaviour and of the impossibility for man to remain untainted by evil.

He has a little in common with all the other characters. Ironically, like the ancient colonists who had 'good friends in Rome' (p. 20), like the manager and Kurtz, he obtains his post through recommendation, and is involved, even against his will, in a struggle for power, as Kurtz's comment 'I am glad' (p. 77) shows. Like Kurtz, he is represented 'as an exceptional and gifted creature' (p. 27) and an 'emissary of light' (p. 27). He is aware, however, that this makes him an 'impostor' (p. 27), which suggests that one cannot serve colonialism without being corrupted by it. He too resembles 'an idol' (p. 18) and is several times compared to a Buddha either 'preaching in European clothes' (p. 21), which naturally recalls Kurtz, or alternately 'meditating' (p. 95), which may convey the wisdom he has attained. Like Kurtz (p. 47), he prefers at one stage to turn to the wilderness (p. 79) rather than face the manager's particular evil. He is not without his own contradictions as, for instance, when he declares 'Mr. Kurtz was no idol of mine' (p. 75) yet shortly afterwards admits that he had 'to invoke him – himself – his own exalted and incredible degradation' (p. 83) as if Kurtz were some kind of evil god that had to be placated. His most obvious contradiction is when he says he detests and can't bear a lie (p. 42) yet lies first to the brickmaker, and is aware of being a 'pretence' (p. 42) then, more significantly, he lies to Kurtz's Intended. Tearing off the postscript from Kurtz's report is also a kind of lie.

These contradictions indicate that Joseph Conrad creates human beings as they are, not as they ought to be; also that each situation demands a new choice and not a blind adherence to a code. Certainly Marlow appears as a balanced and positive character, equally distrustful of self-righteousness and claims to superiority. He is sensitive and humane, a man who knows his own mind and rejects both the white man's exploitation of the natives and his loss of self-control when, like other Conradian characters, he is confronted with the unknown.

Nevertheless, since Chinua Achebe's now famous diatribe against Joseph Conrad's 'racism' (see Critical History) Marlow is often said to express the author's prejudices. In this respect, your interpretation will depend on a close reading of the text, bringing together and comparing passages that will help you choose your own interpretation and answer the question: does Marlow really consider Africa as the seat of evil and Africans as inferior beings? Or does he see both Europeans and Africans as equally susceptible to good and evil? Whatever the answer, Marlow pleads for authenticity (one's 'own true stuff') and this is linked with his moral awareness. His main role in the narrative is, to use Joseph Conrad's words in his preface to *The Nigger of the Narcissus*, to make us '*see*', and indeed the reader sometimes sees more than Marlow himself – which prevents him/her, for instance, from sharing Marlow's admiration for the accountant and, possibly, for Kurtz's 'moral victory'. Marlow's instrument, like Kurtz's, is his eloquence. Just as he keeps referring to Kurtz as 'little more than a voice' (pp. 64 and 77), so the first narrator says of him that he was 'no more … than a voice' (p. 43). Like Marlow, the reader must learn to discriminate between a gift which is used to exalt yet deceive (as Kurtz does) and a gift which is used to give pleasure and edify.

KURTZ

Kurtz may be said to represent the best and the worst of all that the white man is capable. His portrait is built up long before he actually appears in the narrative. Everyone is full of him. The accountant at the Outer Station calls him 'a very remarkable person', though, when further questioned, he only adds that Kurtz 'Sends in as much ivory as all the others put together' (p. 34). At the Central Station the brickmaker calls him (with a mixture of hate and envy) 'a special being' and an 'emissary of pity, and science, and progress, and devil knows what else' (p. 40). He is said to belong to the 'gang of virtue' and, before he meets him, Marlow admires his humanitarianism and romantic idealism, though he is curious to find out how Kurtz's 'moral ideas' (p. 46) will stand the test of experience. The first real glimpse he has of Kurtz is provided by an image to which he (and the reader) responds imaginatively, that of Kurtz turning his back 'on the headquarters ... on thoughts of home ... setting his face towards the depths of the wilderness' (p. 47). This image sums up what has happened to Kurtz. But it is only when Marlow sees the shrunken heads on poles that his former image of Kurtz suddenly collapses.

Kurtz's idealism and desire to bring the light of white civilisation to Africa are inseparable from his inordinate pride and will-to-power. This applies to him both as an individual and as an agent of Europe, which takes its own superiority for granted. His many gifts as a musician, a painter, a journalist, and a politician make him truly representative of a highly sophisticated culture but also of the eurocentric belief in its own universal superiority. He is an arch-egoist and keeps talking to Marlow of '*My* Intended, *my* ivory, *my* station, *my* river' (p. 65, italics mine. See also p. 85). Joseph Conrad once wrote that 'A man haunted by a fixed idea is insane. He is dangerous even if that idea is the idea of justice'. He alludes here to the perversion of idealism that inevitably follows the obstinate and uncontrolled wish to achieve one's ends. Marlow is appalled to discover human heads on the fence surrounding Kurtz's station, to hear that he took part in 'unspeakable rites' (p. 66) and that he was prepared to kill the harlequin, who has saved his life, for a little ivory. He attributes the transformation of virtue into vice in Kurtz to his lack of 'restraint' and adds 'there was something wanting in him – some small matter which, when the pressing need arose, could not be found under his magnificent eloquence' (p. 74). The suggestion here is that Kurtz's love of words is not matched by a moral sense which could save him in moments of crisis; it has become a mere façade hiding a hollowness which is different from the manager's in that the latter had no ideal to begin with. Hence the contradiction in his report between the expression of 'every altruistic sentiment' and 'Exterminate all the brutes!' (p. 66), a contradiction which illustrates the unavoidable ambivalence of imperialism. Hence also Marlow's own description of Kurtz's eloquence in ambivalent terms (p. 63) and his contradictory reaction to it, saying in one place 'It made me tingle with enthusiasm' (p. 66) but calling the memory of it 'one immense jabber ... without any kind of sense' (p. 64).

Kurtz remains a divided being to the last. He ordered the attack to be launched on the whites, but when they reach the station he lets them take him away and prevents the tribesmen from launching another attack. Once on the boat he leaves it to join the tribesmen; but when Marlow comes for him, he does not make the row that might lead to a massacre of the whites. Until just before dying he is a self-deceived idealist, yet seems to be engaged in a personal contest with the wilderness: 'Oh, but I will wring your heart yet!' he exclaims. And Marlow insists that up to the moment of death he struggled with himself (pp. 83 and 85). By wanting to become a god and giving up all restraint he has actually become a devil, a slave to the wilderness (in his heart and in the forest) which he intended to subdue. In Kurtz, Joseph Conrad points to the danger of spiritual pride, of presuming that man can measure himself against forces he cannot even gauge.

What is to be our final assessment of Kurtz? Marlow says that 'Whatever he was, he was not common' (p. 67). He repeats several times that Kurtz is a remarkable man (pp. 79, 87 and 92) because of his extraordinary gifts, because he is at least involved in a spiritual struggle, which the manager and his pilgrims ignore or despise, and because his final cry shows that he eventually understands the nature of his perversion. He also says, however, that he was not 'worth the life [that of his helmsman] we lost in getting to him' (p. 67). If we put together all Marlow's comments about Kurtz, we will see that the image we get remains full of contradictions, and this illustrates the good and the evil of which he, like any of us, is capable. It has been suggested that Kurtz is a tragic hero, someone who aspires to a greatness and fulfilment which his human condition prevents him from attaining. But this is to reduce his responsibility for his own degradation and for the total failure of his humanitarian ideals.

THE ACCOUNTANT

The accountant is the first white man Marlow meets when he reaches the Congo. His impeccable outfit offers such a contrast to the dying natives at the 'grove of death' that Marlow at first takes him for a 'miracle' (p. 32), although by calling him 'a hairdresser's dummy' (p. 33), he seems to present an automaton rather than a man. The accountant presents Marlow with one kind of aberration in the so-called civilising enterprise: futile, mechanical and heartless efficiency. Yet Marlow expresses admiration for what he has achieved: with great difficulty he has taught a native woman to clean and starch his collars and shirt-fronts, and his books are in 'apple-pie order' (p. 33). There seems to be no irony in Marlow's admiration, which fits in with his respect for efficient work. Joseph Conrad, however, makes sure we do not share it by contrasting ironically the accountant's immaculate clothing with the muddle around him, and above all by showing in what way he illustrates the 'philanthropic pretence'. His complete blindness to the horrors of the 'grove of death' when he comes out 'to get a breath of fresh air' (p. 33) and his indifference to, even impatience with, the sufferings of the dying agent, reveal his egoism and insensitiveness. In his vanity and hatred of the natives he anticipates Kurtz, whom he so much admires. He is self-controlled and competent only at the cost of his dehumanisation.

THE MANAGER AND HIS 'FAITHLESS PILGRIMS'

The manager is Marlow's other 'choice of nightmares' (p. 79), whose cynicism contrasts with Kurtz's self-deceptive idealism. Unlike Kurtz, he is a commonplace man with 'no genius ... no learning, and no intelligence' (p. 37), who can only keep the routine going but 'originate[s] nothing'. His ineptitude is an ironic comment on the civilisers' claim to intellectual and technological superiority. He has reached his position only because he is never ill. Marlow explains that his endurance is due to his inner emptiness: 'Perhaps there was nothing within him' (p. 37). His hollowness is positively evil, the expression of his amorality. Marlow's feeling that the manager is capable of anything inspires him with uneasiness. His impression is confirmed when the manager countenances his uncle's assertion that 'Anything – anything can be done in this country' (p. 48). He has not waited for his uncle's cynical comment, 'The climate may do away with this difficulty [Kurtz] for you' (p. 47), to make sure that it does. He has probably sunk the steamer intentionally just before Marlow's arrival and he sees to it that Marlow does not get the rivets to repair it, thus further delaying the rescue of Kurtz. In addition, the manager would kill the harlequin if he found him too troublesome.

With those of his kind the manager cynically denies all human values, as when he refers to the 'pestiferous absurdity' of Kurtz's talk (p. 48). He does not object to Kurtz's exploitation of the natives in order to get ivory and calls his method 'unsound' (p. 78) only out of sheer envy. However deluded Kurtz may be, one can at least believe in his sincerity. The manager is not only an intriguer (see his conversation with his uncle) but a hypocrite. He pretends to be anxious about Kurtz's illness (p. 37). Though the rescue of Kurtz is a pretence, the manager wants to preserve appearances, the only 'restraint' of which he is capable. His comment to Marlow 'I authorise you to take all the risks' when he knows Marlow must refuse, contradicts his later statement 'Cautiously, cautiously – that's my principle' (p. 78). He can say anything because he has no inner conviction, and his mean-spirited comments on Kurtz create 'an atmosphere so vile' (p. 79) on the boat that Marlow turns for relief to the wilderness.

The absence of any real sense of responsibility in the manager is reflected in the behaviour of his agents, whom Marlow ironically calls 'faithless' and 'bewitched' pilgrims. Indeed, their behaviour is a parody of the purposefulness that ought to inspire what white men saw as their 'mission' to civilise Africa. With long staves in their hands they '[stroll] aimlessly about in the sunshine' (p. 38), and they revere ivory like an idol: 'You would think they were praying to it' (p. 38). They serve, in fact, the 'flabby, pretending, weak-eyed devil of a rapacious and pitiless folly' (p. 31) which presides over the colonialist enterprise. They too are 'hollow men' behaving with cowardice and madness, as when they fire blindly into the bush when they reach the Inner Station. These men are responsible for 'the great demoralisation of the land' (p. 33). No wonder Marlow sees their station and everything about them as 'unreal' (p. 38).

The members of the Eldorado Exploring Expedition can be compared to the pilgrims although they are, if possible, even worse. 'Their talk ... was the talk of sordid buccaneers: it was reckless without hardihood, greedy without audacity, and cruel without courage' (p. 46). Joseph

Conrad's use of the terms 'Eldorado' and 'buccaneers' clearly links these men with the New World conquerors who were hoping to find an 'El Dorado' in South America (like Sir Walter Raleigh) and with the buccaneers of various European nations who were merely thieves of Central America's riches. The leader of the expedition, the manager's uncle, is a cynic without scruples who helps his nephew in his intrigues and bluntly hopes that the jungle will kill Kurtz.

THE BRICKMAKER

He is one of the 'pilgrims' but stands out among them as a particularly striking example of their uselessness. He is supposed to make bricks but has been at the station for more than a year just waiting for the necessary material, 'backbiting and intriguing' (p. 39) like his fellow agents, who think he is 'the manager's spy upon them' (p. 39). He seems to be in league with his superior and to receive special treatment. In his hut there is a silver-mounted dressing case and a whole candle, while no-one else is entitled to them; an empty champagne bottle; and some African trophies, which suggests that he has already ransacked the land for pieces of African art. He is an aristocrat but vulgar in his purposes and the means used to reach them. He wants to become assistant-manager not through merit but by intrigue, and shamelessly pumps Marlow about his acquaintances in Brussels, feeling threatened by him as much as by Kurtz.

The brickmaker could be taken as a parody of Kurtz. He pays lip service to Kurtz's ideals and declaims, that is, he repeats in a theatrical and rhetorical manner the eloquent words of idealists without meaning them at all. When a fire breaks out at night and creates an inferno-like background enhanced by the groans of a beaten negro, the brickmaker appears to Marlow as a 'papier-mâché Mephistopheles' (p. 41), which fits in with the farcical pretensions of the cause he supposedly serves. With his 'forked little beard and a hooked nose' (p. 39) he has the appearance of one, too. Kurtz, who has 'taken a high seat amongst the devils of the land' (p. 65), must at least be taken seriously. In the presence of this other 'hollow man' Marlow is the more impressed by the powerful reality of the jungle: 'All this was great, expectant, mute, while the man jabbered about himself' (p. 42).

THE HARLEQUIN

The harlequin is Marlow's most enigmatic encounter in the jungle. His first perception of the kind of man the harlequin may be is given to him through the book he has left behind, *An Inquiry into some Points of Seamanship*. In its 'honest concern for the right way of going to work' (p. 53) Marlow detects a foil to the surrounding wilderness. The harlequin has indeed survived without apparently being touched by it. Like Marlow, he is efficient, wholly self-reliant, and has carefully planned his escape from the Inner Station. He is, however, an ambiguous character. Smiles and frowns, sunshine and shadow alternate on his face. His youth seems to be a virtue in itself and the secret of his capacity for survival:

> The glamour of youth enveloped his parti-coloured rags, his destitution, his loneliness, the essential desolation of his futile wanderings … there he was gallantly, thoughtlessly alive, to all appearances indestructible solely by the virtue of his few years and of his unreflecting audacity. (p. 71)

Like Marlow, the harlequin is fascinated by Kurtz. But his devotion to him is blind and morally naive: 'He had not meditated over it … and he accepted it with a sort of eager fatalism' (p. 71). His uneasiness while talking to Marlow about Kurtz's exploits shows that he senses Kurtz's perversity but cannot judge it. When piqued by Marlow's teasing, he can only say vaguely 'He made me see things – things' (p. 72), which amounts to saying that he could see nothing, and is a sign of his immaturity. He idolises Kurtz in the same way as the natives and, in Marlow's words, 'crawled as much as the veriest savage of them all' (p. 75). Just as he keeps saying about the natives 'They are simple people' (pp. 69 and 79), he says about himself 'I am a simple man' (pp. 75 and 80).

The harlequin seems to have much in common with the fool or trickster who appears in all literary traditions, whether Renaissance English drama, Italian *commedia dell'arte*, American-Indian or African folk-tales. As his parti-coloured rags suggest, he is a man without a fixed identity and therefore adaptable, who eludes the tyrannies of the established order (such as the manager and his acolytes represent) thanks to his cunning and occasional humour. In his pre-social and fluid state he seems to embody all possibilities of human development.

THE NATIVES

Marlow's approach to the natives reflects Joseph Conrad's outlook, i.e. admiration partly overshadowed by the prejudices of the period in which he wrote. The first example of this duality occurs when Marlow comments on the negroes he sees along the African coast: 'they had faces like grotesque masks ... but they had bone, muscle, a wild vitality, an intense energy of movement, that was as natural and true as the surf along their coast' (p. 28). The reference to 'grotesque masks' is as pejorative and offensive nowadays as Marlow's portrait of the fireman as 'a dog in a parody of breeches and a feather hat, walking on his hind-legs' (p. 52), though no more so than comparing white men to monkeys on a tight-rope or his reference to his own monkey tricks (p. 50). Marlow's use of the word 'nigger', generally accepted at the end of the nineteenth century, is also offensive today. Yet Marlow admires the natives who still fit into their environment and have preserved their cultural identity, like Kurtz's black mistress, but he comments disparagingly on those who have become detribalised, the 'reclaimed' (p. 30) who imitate the white man, like the leader of the chained slave gang at the 'grove of death'.

    Marlow does not make the mistake of confusing all Africans as white people often do even now. He discriminates between the tribes who live and work in their country of origin, like the cannibals, and the Africans who have been brought in from the coast and (like the white man) are 'lost in uncongenial surroundings, fed on unfamiliar food' (p. 32), and therefore sicken and become inefficient. He is indignant at the way 'men – men, I tell you' (p. 31) are being treated. Another example of Marlow's ambivalent attitude towards Africans is his presentation of the so-called 'cannibals'. Marlow calls them cannibals but offers no proof that they are, only saying that they were prepared to eat the dead helmsman and later the blacks of the Inner Station firing at the steamboat. However, he genuinely admires the cannibals' self-possession and their restraint when they are very hungry, asserting, clearly about men generally, that 'No fear can stand up to hunger ... disgust simply does not exist where hunger is ... and as to superstition, beliefs, and what you may call principles, they are less than chaff in a breeze' (p. 57). Marlow also calls the cannibals his friends, though this may also sound paternalistic. Marlow's appreciation of the natives, however, seems to be implicitly denied later by his lie to Kurtz's Intended.

THE HELMSMAN

Like the fireman, he is a detribalized African, an 'improved specimen' (p. 52), says Marlow ironically, who has come from the coast and been trained by Fresleven. He has thus been cut off from his own community and has lost the dignity and the 'inborn strength' characteristic of the inland natives. As a result he has become 'unstable', foolishly proud one moment and abjectly frightened the next. When the steamboat is attacked by Kurtz's followers, he loses his self-control completely and becomes like 'a tree [swayed] by the wind' (pp. 61 and 67). His frantic behaviour contrasts with the 'fierce and steady' expression of their assailants. He is responsible for his own death since he was wounded by a spear after opening the shutter of the pilot-house. His inquiring glance as he dies seems to express his confusion and disorientation, though the reality he has denied appears to take over again as his glance acquires a 'sombre, brooding, and menacing expression' (p. 62). The scene of his death anticipates the other confrontation between black and white values that plays itself out when Kurtz dies. Marlow deplores the fact that, like Kurtz, 'He had no restraint, no restraint' (p. 67) and laments his death because of the subtle bond created between them by their work together.

KURTZ'S NATIVE MISTRESS

Kurtz's African mistress is a kind of black muse, the living spirit of primitive Africa and of its 'fecund and mysterious life' (p. 77). Marlow first sees her as 'a wild and gorgeous apparition' (p. 77). He presents her in the same ambivalent terms as he does the jungle: 'She was savage and superb, wild-eyed and magnificent' and, like the wilderness itself (see p. 49), she has 'an air of brooding over an inscrutable purpose' (p. 77). She is the 'tenebrous and passionate soul' (p. 77) of the land and exerts on Kurtz the same mixture of fascination and repulsion. This is obvious when he faces her for the last time and looks at her and all she represents 'with a mingled expression of wistfulness and hate' (p. 84). She is unimpressed by the white men and shows more dignity than they do, as when she alone does not so much as flinch when Marlow pulls the string of the boat's whistle.

The harlequin clearly resents her power and accuses her of trying to persuade Kurtz to kill him (the harlequin). When she opens her arms 'the swift shadows darted out on the earth … gathering the steamer into a shadowy embrace' (p. 78). This gesture, repeated at the time of departure (p. 84), seems to express her attempt to keep possession of Kurtz's soul, fighting the invisible white muse (the Intended) who struggles for his possession too. Although Marlow is repelled by the unspeakable rites in which his African mistress may have participated with Kurtz, the words he uses to describe her, 'gorgeous', 'magnificent', 'superb', show his admiration for the dynamic energy she symbolises. She too is 'truth stripped of its cloak of time' (p. 52), whereas the Intended is all self-deception.

THE INTENDED

She is, like her name, largely symbolic, for she represents the *intention*, the unchanging, absolute idealism men can imagine but never live up to. It is difficult to think of her as a flesh-and-blood woman who loves a real man more than the ideas he expounds. But if we keep in mind what she is supposed to represent, the deadness and illusory greatness of Western civilisation, her presentation is a masterpiece of ambiguity. She has the qualities Marlow most admires: 'A mature capacity for fidelity, for belief, for suffering' (p. 91). Marlow reads a 'delicate shade of truthfulness' (p. 90) and altruism upon her features. Her surroundings, however, are essentially dead (see Imagery); she lives in a graveyard supported by a 'saving illusion' (p. 93) and a lie. The fact that Marlow should see Kurtz, in his voracious aspect, enter her house with him, and that during their conversation he should see them together and hear the whisper of his last cry, shows that they are indissociable.

   For all the clarity of her ideals, Marlow feels he has 'blundered into a place of cruel and absurd mysteries' (p. 92). Nowhere better than here does he show that the light she supposedly represents is actually a source of death, as her 'ashy halo' (p. 91) suggests. Marlow says that she, too, was just a voice (p. 64) and during their interview she 'talked' and 'talked' (p. 92). She clearly manoeuvres Marlow into telling her what she wants to hear, and this shows the extent of her self-deception and perhaps a refusal to know the truth. It is as if she kept the wilderness alive by refusing to recognise its existence. Note the irony at the end of the following passage, in which the words of the girl merge with the reality Kurtz has experienced in the jungle:

> the sound of her low voice seemed to have the accompaniment of all the other
> sounds, full of mystery, desolation, and sorrow, I had ever heard – the ripple of the
> river … the murmurs of the crowds … the whisper of a voice speaking from beyond
> the threshold of an eternal darkness. 'But you have heard him! You know!' she cried.
> (p. 93)

This implies that the light of idealism is inseparable from the darkness of actual life. In the course of the interview the Intended comes increasingly to resemble her opposite, the African mistress. She is possessive like her and exclaims 'he needed me! Me!' (p. 94). She too stretches out her arms as after a retreating figure, and her cry of 'inconceivable triumph and unspeakable pain' (p. 94) recalls the native woman's 'tragic and fierce aspect' (p. 77). Beside her, however, the Intended seems unsubstantial, a mere 'shade' (p. 94). We saw that the discrepancy between the idealism she upholds and the darkness of his moral decay is probably part of Kurtz's discovery when he cries out 'The horror! The horror!'. The final irony in the novel (whether intended by Joseph Conrad or not, we shall never know) may be that Kurtz's last cry *is* her name and a desperate pronouncement on the spuriousness of one-sided idealism.

THE MINOR CHARACTERS

THE KNITTERS OF BLACK WOOL
Their 'indifferent placidity' and 'unconcerned wisdom' (p. 25) disturb Marlow, who feels they know all about him. Their role seems largely symbolic. The older one, 'guarding the door of Darkness' is 'scrutinising the cheery and foolish faces with unconcerned old eyes' (p. 25). Marlow thinks of her when he goes ashore after Kurtz (p. 81) and is on the point of struggling with the unknown in himself. Because they seem 'uncanny and fateful' (p. 25) and knit continuously, they are often taken for the Fates, in classical mythology, goddesses who spin the thread of man's life and determine its course.

THE COMPANY'S CLERK
He has a drink with Marlow while they are waiting to go to the doctor's. His sententious comments about those who are foolish enough to go to Africa link him with the petty and ignorant people Marlow meets in the streets of Brussels on his return from Africa.

CHARACTERISATION continued

THE DOCTOR

He is a pseudo-scientist, who measures the skulls of those who go 'out there' and finds 'the mental changes of individuals' (p. 26) interesting for science, though he never sees the agents when they return. This may mean that he is not interested in seeing them or, ominously, that most do not come back. There is more truth in what he says than he seems to be aware of, particularly in his assertion that 'the changes take place inside' (p. 26). This implies that each man has inner depths to be explored and that to do so may be dangerous. The mechanical inquiries of the doctor and his obvious indifference to the men under his scrutiny are in keeping with the enterprise he serves and add to Marlow's uneasiness. In the African interior he appropriately remembers the doctor's advice: *'Du calme, du calme'* (p. 27).

THE AUNT

Her misguided conception of Marlow's 'mission' is inspired by what she has read in newspapers and which Marlow calls 'rot' (p. 27). She remains totally impervious to Marlow's assertion that the company is run for profit. Marlow treats her with ironic affection, emphasising her lack of realism which he sees as typical of women: 'It's queer how out of touch with truth women are' (p. 27), he says, a statement which also applies to the Intended. Her recommendations when Marlow leaves and is 'told to wear flannel [in a tropical country!], be sure to write often, and so on' (p. 27) are ridiculous in the light of the very real physical and moral dangers he faces but of which she is totally unaware. Marlow's statement that men should help women 'to stay in that beautiful world of their own' (p. 64) is, of course, nowadays sharply and relevantly denounced by feminist critics as a misogynous and patriarchal judgement.

THEMES

Heart of Darkness is the first of Joseph Conrad's novels or stories that achieves the complexity of a great work of art. Its implications are individual, social, political and metaphysical. It can be read as a tale of adventure as, it seems, most of Joseph Conrad's tales were read by his early, contemporary readers. Marlow recalls his (and, as we know, Conrad's) passionate interest as a boy in 'the glories of exploration' (p. 22), in

cartography, and his particular fascination with the then blank spaces of
the earth, especially the North Pole and the Congo. His tale then offers
a faithful if 'impressionistic' account of his journey (see Narrative
Technique). Even before that, however, he has introduced the major
subject of his story in his very first words by saying that Britain was once
'one of the dark places of the earth' (p. 19) and by referring to its
colonisation by the Romans. The two paragraphs in which he evokes
Roman imperialism prefigure the whole narrative and presents its major
themes in a nutshell: the colonisation of distant, unknown countries and its
attendant evils, the moral test to which the colonisers, as individuals, were
subjected (the 'fascination of the abomination' – p. 21), and the philosophical reflection generated by that test ('we live in the flicker' – p. 20).

COLONIALISM

Increasingly, in the last twenty years or so, *Heart of Darkness* has been read
not only as an inquiry into the nature of colonialism and a severe
denunciation of it but as an illustration of Joseph Conrad's own ambivalent
attitude towards imperialism (see Critical History). At the same time it
questions the value of white civilisation and the desirability of its
transplantation to what were then considered as 'primitive' countries. As
Marlow indirectly suggests by referring to the Roman conquest,
colonialism has existed since the earliest times of human history. One of the
merits of the novel is to present colonialism not as a political and economic
venture only, but as a consequence of the individual's lust for power and
possessiveness and even as an epitome of man's capacity for evil.

Early in the narrative Joseph Conrad presents approaches to
colonialism that prevailed when he wrote the novel. The anonymous
narrator sees it only as a glorious adventure, at once an expression of
England's greatness and a means of adding to it. He is not aware that by
calling English conquerors 'hunters for gold or pursuers of fame' (p. 19) he
associates them with the Roman invaders who 'grabbed what they could for
the sake of what was to be got' (p. 21) and with all the characters in
Marlow's tale who take part in the colonialist enterprise for selfish
purposes. Nor does he realise that by pointing to the two symbols of that
enterprise, 'the sword' and 'the torch' (p. 19), he is actually referring to
brutal force and to the negation of native culture by the so-called light of

civilisation. His view of imperialism was naturally widespread at the end of the nineteenth century, but it is clear that, at this stage at least, like the harlequin, the first narrator has not 'meditated over it' (p. 71). Similarly, Marlow's aunt has an idealistic view of colonialism and is pleased with herself for helping to send Marlow to Africa as one of the 'Workers' and as an 'emissary of light' (p. 27). She subscribes entirely to the view that the motive behind colonialism is to civilise the conquered peoples, 'weaning those ignorant millions from their horrid ways' (p. 27). Her conception of the colonialist intention corresponds to that expressed by Rudyard Kipling in a poem called 'The White Man's Burden', which emphasises the ideals of duty and service ('To serve your captives' need') that inspired many who went to the colonies but also expressed their prejudiced view of the colonised: 'Your new-caught, sullen peoples, half-devil and half-child'.

Although Marlow's mission is limited to the rescue of Kurtz, there is a sense in which his trip to the Congo is itself a recreation of the colonialist expedition. His definition of colonialism is ambivalent since he asserts that it is 'redeemed' by the idea at the back of it. We should wonder to what extent this dualistic view is substantiated by the narrative and by Marlow's confrontation with its reality. Already on his way out to Africa he notices that the only settlements seen from the coast are trading places with names out of some 'sordid farce' (p. 28) while he thinks there is 'a touch of insanity' (p. 29) about the man-of-war firing into the continent. Even at this early stage the colonial expedition strikes him as a 'merry dance of death and trade' (p. 29) or as 'a weary pilgrimage amongst hints for nightmares' (p. 29). Not until he comes to the 'grove of death', however, does he realise the full extent of the destructive process in which the whites are engaged in Africa, and the misgivings he has had in Brussels and on his journey along the African coast are confirmed. His suspicion that he will become acquainted with 'a flabby, pretending, weak-eyed devil of a rapacious and pitiless folly' (p. 31) is also immediately confirmed when he comes upon the dying negroes.

What he ironically calls 'the work!' (p. 32) is an irrational and meaningless violation of the land and its people. The transplantation of the trappings of white civilisation (the boiler and the railway-truck) and of a type of behaviour specific to it (the blasting on the hillside, the accountant's well-kept books, the 'law' which remains a mystery to the natives) seems to make no sense here. No effort is made by the colonialists to understand the

alien population that they exploit as 'raw matter' (p. 30). The horror
Marlow experiences reaches a climax when he comes upon natives too tired
or too ill to work and merely left to die. Again, the words used to describe
them – 'shapes', 'bundles of acute angles', 'phantoms' – eloquently express
the fact that these men have been reduced to mere objects, squeezed out of
life through hard labour, then discarded. Just as the setting offers a picture
of devastation, so the condition and posture of the men suggest 'a massacre
and a pestilence' (p. 32). This prevalence of death among men in the
ravaged forest gives Marlow the impression that he has entered some
gloomy inferno. As Marlow's insistence on blackness, disease and death
indicates, it is not light but darkness the white man has brought with him,
unless it be the false light radiated by the accountant.

Marlow then first discovers the effects of imperialism in the 'grove of
death' before discovering at the Inner Station how the white man is led to
behave with such indifferent cruelty. But first when he sets out for the
Central Station, he is made to see into the real motives that bring many a
white man to Africa. His travelling companion, who keeps fainting in the
heat, tells him that 'of course' he has come to make money (p. 35). The
manager is a 'common trader' (p. 36) and his agents have turned ivory into
a god. Their hatred of Kurtz as a successful collector of ivory points to the
corrupting influence of their enterprise. As to the members of the Eldorado
Exploring Expedition, their unashamed desire is 'to tear treasure out of the
bowels of the land … with no more moral purpose at the back of it than
there is in burglars breaking into a safe' (p. 46).

Before Marlow actually meets him, Kurtz seems to be a very different
kind of colonialist since even his detractors acknowledge that he is an
idealist and that he has come out 'equipped with moral ideas' (p. 46). He
remains a self-deceived idealist to the very end. Yet he has become a
ruthless exploiter, who is prepared to kill for a little ivory. Instead of turning
his station into 'a beacon on the road towards better things', as he intended
to do, 'a centre … for humanising, improving, instructing' (p. 48), he has
given in to the 'fascination of the abomination' (p. 21), as his participation
in 'unspeakable rites' (p. 66) and the human heads on the poles around his
house indicate. While gradually building up the personality of Kurtz for his
listeners, Marlow exposes the contradiction inherent in colonialism, i.e. the
discrepancy between the Europeans' words, particularly their public
utterances, and their actions. The contrast between Kurtz's 'burning noble

words' and the criminal postscript to his report 'Exterminate all the brutes!' (p. 66) is a stroke of genius, for this is what reveals the extent of Kurtz's self-deception and the failure of white civilisation to put its ideals into practice. More than that, it shows the perversion of those ideals. White civilisation has been tested and found wanting.

Why then does Marlow say that the 'idea' at the back of colonialism redeems it? Admittedly, after drawing attention to the white man's limitations and exposing his sense of superiority as sham, he calls it an 'illusion' (p. 93) but a 'great and saving' illusion to which he bows his head as if it were an idol or a fetish. Why does he lie to Kurtz's Intended, not only about Kurtz himself but about the real nature of imperialism? Like much in *Heart of Darkness*, Marlow's lie lends itself to many interpretations. To suggest that he lied out of compassion for the Intended is inadequate, for he does not lie merely to protect her from knowledge. The illusion 'redeems' the rest of the civilised world as well. Marlow's excuse, 'It would have been too dark – too dark altogether' (p. 94), shows that his is a protective lie, and we must remember that earlier in his tale he said 'We must help [women] to stay in that beautiful world of their own, *lest ours gets worse*' (p. 64, italics mine). Several early critics saw the 'illusion' as a positive one, because it offered an alternative to mere corruption or the ignorance of it and at least helped men like Marlow to live up to their ideals of efficiency and restraint and to survive. Recent commentators, however, have criticised Marlow's lie more severely, asserting that, in the end, he covers up the very horrors he has denounced. Another interpretation is that Joseph Conrad himself presents two irreconcilable positions, a denunciation of imperialism yet a reluctant affirmation of imperialist civilisation as represented by the Intended (see Benita Parry in Critical History). Feminist critics are particularly virulent in their criticism of a lie told because women were supposedly unable to face the truth of both imperialism and existence with the same fortitude as men.

One should also keep in mind that Marlow's attitude towards the Africans is not utterly devoid of paternalism. But, on the whole, he systematically undermines the role of white civilisation, exposing its shortcomings and deceptions; while at the same time, by calling Africa and its people an 'enigma', he recognises that they have a specific character which the white man should try to understand. This was revolutionary enough in Joseph Conrad's time and ran counter to ingrained prejudices.

Possibly, Joseph Conrad felt that he could go no further, and he may have
made a concession to his contemporaries by allowing Marlow to insist on
the value of the saving ideal even if it was illusory and at the cost of a lie.

Several critics have asserted that in *Heart of Darkness* Joseph Conrad
criticised Belgian colonialism only, but approved of the work done by the
British in their colonies. Apart from what is known of Conrad's admiration
for the British, their argument is that when Marlow looks at a map of the
world in the company's office, he comments: 'There was a vast amount of
red – good to see at any time, because one knows that some real work is
done in there' (p. 24). There is no denying the atrocious conditions of
Belgian colonisation nor their impact on Joseph Conrad. But to suggest
that Conrad approved of British imperialism or that he condemned one
kind of colonialism and admired another is to restrict the novel's
significance. Marlow's comment is, indeed, belied by his own narrative.
The juxtaposition of the nameless narrator's praise of the greatness of
British conquerors with Marlow's description of Roman colonialism throws
an ironic light on British achievement. Marlow's definition of colonialism
(p. 21) is general and applies to all such enterprises. Kurtz has been
educated partly in England and his mother was half-English. 'All Europe',
says Marlow, 'contributed to the making of Kurtz' (p. 66), and his self-
deception clearly applies to all European imperialism. It is not impossible
that in Marlow's praise of the 'real work' done in British colonies Joseph
Conrad was partly playing up to his audience.

JOURNEY INTO THE SELF AND INTO THE UNCONSCIOUS

Heart of Darkness does not deal exclusively with colonialism. It also
recreates a voyage of self-discovery and is often described as a story of
initiation or, as Albert Guerard puts it, a 'night journey'. How does Joseph
Conrad reconcile the two aspects of Marlow's experience, that is, his
confrontation with the reality of colonialism and an introspective voyage
leading to spiritual change? No doubt one of the story's greatest
achievements is that the actual voyage should, through Joseph Conrad's
symbolic language, evoke a journey into the self. But it is also essential to
realise that Joseph Conrad does not present two separate issues, a public
one (colonialism) and a private one (knowledge of the self). The two are
indissociable, and Marlow's story clearly implies that the kind of world men

make for themselves, and for others, largely results from the character of individual behaviour. For example, Kurtz's will-to-power and that of men like him lies at the core of imperialism, which is also what the manager, his 'faithless pilgrims', and the members of the El Dorado Expedition make it. Like these men, Marlow has been cut off from his original background and faces an alien environment. One essential difference between them and Marlow lies in his awareness that his moral being is subjected to a trial, and in his attempt to understand the significance of his experience.

We must remember that Marlow is present in the narrative from beginning to end. In fact, Kurtz's appearance in the story is comparatively brief, and even then Marlow deals as much with his own reactions to Kurtz as with Kurtz himself. At the beginning of his tale Marlow refers to their meeting as 'the culminating point of my experience. It seemed somehow to throw a kind of light on everything about me – and into my thoughts' (p. 22). When he repairs the steamboat at the Central Station and meditates on the effect of work, he says 'I like what is in the work, – the chance to find yourself. Your own reality ... what no other man can know' (p. 44). And when he returns to Brussels, he is irritated by the complacency of the people he meets in the street, feeling that 'they could not possibly know the things [he] knew' (p. 88).

Marlow's trip from Europe to the Outer, then to the Central Station already tests his capacity to discriminate between good and evil since he witnesses actions that elicit a moral judgement from him, such as the futile firing of a man-of-war into the African continent, and what amounts to genocide at the 'grove of death'. His detailed account of what he sees there shows his compassion, which contrasts with the accountant's indifference and fits of hatred. There also he hears of Kurtz for the first time and from then on becomes gradually obsessed with a desire to meet him. When they finally leave for the Inner Station, Marlow says 'For me it [the boat] crawled towards Kurtz – exclusively' (p. 51). Immediately afterwards he declares 'We penetrated deeper and deeper into the heart of darkness' (p. 51). This conjunction of Kurtz with the heart of darkness sums up the ultimate purpose of Marlow's exploration. In the course of his journey up-river the narrative acquires an increasingly symbolical meaning, and the landscape becomes a psychological as much as a physical reality. This is conveyed by Marlow's insistence that the 'earth seemed unearthly' (p. 51) and that his experience has a dream-like quality, as well as by a growing impression that they lose the support of the material world. 'We were cut off from the comprehension of our surroundings' (p. 51), says Marlow, and further 'The rest of the world was nowhere, as far as our eyes and ears were concerned. Just nowhere' (p. 56). They are by then surrounded by a thick fog which makes them deaf and blind (p. 55), and this obliteration of the senses symbolically anticipates the moral situation in which Kurtz has placed himself at the Inner Station (named symbolically too). Indeed, Marlow calls him an 'initiated wraith from the back of Nowhere' (pp. 65–6). When he actually fights with him, he explains that Kurtz 'had kicked himself loose of the earth ... He was alone, and I before him did not know whether I stood on the ground or floated in the air' (p. 83), which suggests that they have lost the support of the outer world and must fall back on their inner resources in their moral struggle.

We saw that as Marlow penetrates further into the unknown, his capacity for self-control and 'inborn strength' are tested. His real trial, however, only takes place when he feels he has been 'transported into some lightless region of subtle horrors' (p. 75) which Kurtz seems to inhabit. Kurtz is repeatedly described as a shadow, and when Marlow tries to convey the essence of his experience, he declares 'I am trying to account to myself for – for – Mr. Kurtz – for the shade of Mr. Kurtz' (p. 65). Though Kurtz exists as a character in his own right, there is a sense in which he is also Marlow's shadow or 'double'. By declaring that Kurtz is 'a remarkable man' (p. 79) Marlow was lumped together with him, and this identification with the 'nightmare of [his] choice' (p. 81) leads to his confrontation with him. It accounts for the 'moral shock' Marlow receives when he realises that Kurtz has left the steamboat to join the natives; and for his statement 'I was anxious to deal with this shadow by myself alone – and to this day I don't know why I was so jealous of sharing with any one the peculiar blackness of that experience' (p. 81). When Marlow states 'I confounded the beat of the drum with the beating of my heart' (p. 81), he shows that, like Kurtz, he has reached the heart of darkness, 'the farthest point of navigation' (p. 22). It is no longer with the wilderness outside that Marlow fights, but rather with its effect on Kurtz and the spell it cast over him. 'If anybody ever struggled with a soul', he says, 'I am the man' (p. 83). That Marlow's involvement with Kurtz amounts to a plunge into the depths of the self is confirmed when he explains that Kurtz's soul had 'looked within itself, and ... gone mad. I had ... to go through the ordeal of looking into it myself'

(p. 83). Whatever Marlow's arguments, he not only succeeds in bringing Kurtz back to the boat, but remains sufficiently detached to judge with precision the extent of his self-deception, the fact that Kurtz still hides 'in the magnificent folds of eloquence the barren darkness of his heart' (p. 85).

Marlow himself does not achieve complete self-knowledge. This, he says, 'comes too late' (p. 87) at the moment of death. But he comes as near to it as is possible when he witnesses Kurtz's confrontation with death and, after the 'veil has been rent' (p. 86), hears him exclaim 'The horror! The horror!' (p. 86). That is why he says 'It is *his* extremity that I seem to have lived through' (p. 87, italics mine). He interprets this exclamation as 'a judgement upon the adventures of his soul on this earth' (p. 87). He also asserts that 'it had candour, it had conviction … it had the appalling face of a glimpsed truth' (p. 87, see Theme on A Glimpsed Truth). Thus when he steps 'over the threshold of the invisible' (p. 88), Kurtz possibly achieves at last awareness of what he is. Hence Marlow's affirmation that his cry is 'a moral victory' (p. 88), implying that he has discovered some general truth about humankind. As to Marlow, who also struggled with death but only 'peeped over the edge' (p. 87), he found that, were he really to die, he would have nothing to say. His experience, however, seems to have shattered all his former assumptions about humankind. Already in the short story *An Outpost of Progress* Joseph Conrad had stated that 'the contact with pure unmitigated savagery … excites the imagination' and shown in what way it is challenged and tried. After his return from the Congo Marlow comments: 'it was my imagination that wanted soothing' (p. 88), which clearly suggests that his imaginative power and the capacity for moral discrimination that influences it have been sorely tried.

However, the journey into the self can entail not just an examination of one's conscious moral behaviour and thought but also a voyage into the deeper recesses of the psyche: the unconscious which psychoanalysts like Sigmund Freud and Carl Gustav Jung considered as so influential on our behaviour. When individuals are confronted with these depths of the inner self, they become aware of forces which, in their normal state, they ignore or manage to control. These mysterious and normally repressed forces can be considered as the essence of the self which manifests itself in dreams or in a state of strain. It links humanity with the archetypal, primordial and the unknown in the universe. The unconscious acts as an incentive to our actions and thoughts, both good and evil, though as he progresses in the jungle Marlow seems to think increasingly of the unconscious as evil. That Marlow might be setting on a journey into the unconscious is already suggested by the doctor who tells him that 'the changes take place inside' (p. 26). On the voyage out, Africa is presented as an enigma, a continent which might stand for an inner reality to be explored 'smiling, frowning, inviting, grand, mean, insipid, or savage, and always mute, with an air of whispering, Come and find out' (p. 28). At the Central Station, he feels 'its mystery, its greatness, the amazing reality of its concealed life' (p. 41). When he sets out for the interior to meet Kurtz, he says 'going up that river was like travelling back to the earliest beginnings of the world' (p. 49). There is thus a repeated emphasis on his voyage as an exploration of the mysterious and the primordial, the 'rioting invasion of soundless life' (p. 45). This is enhanced by the impressive muteness of the land, occasionally broken by the wild noises of the natives, and by the sense of unreality and dream Marlow experiences as he travels further into the interior.

The novel suggests that those who are incapable of controlling their unconscious run the danger of becoming mad. Unlike the hollow pilgrims Marlow has sufficient consciousness to realise he is often tempted to give in to the wilderness outside and within himself. When, for example, he thinks he will have rivets, he momentarily loses his self-control and behaves like a lunatic with the foreman. It is in Kurtz, however, that the confrontation with the unconscious is fully illustrated. Marlow points out that Kurtz has undergone 'some devilish initiation' (p. 64), and the harlequin tells Marlow that Kurtz would 'forget himself' (p. 73) among the natives. By thus forgetting himself, Kurtz has come face to face with his unconscious and liberated himself from the rules of social life, which Marlow never does. But he becomes a privileged spectator of Kurtz's experience, and his struggle with Kurtz when he goes ashore after him is in a sense a struggle to preserve his own balance and sanity: 'I tried to break ... the heavy, mute spell of the wilderness – that seemed to draw him [Kurtz] to its pitiless breast by the awakening of forgotten and brutal instincts' (pp. 82–3). Kurtz has 'kicked himself loose of the earth' (p. 83). His soul 'had looked within itself, and ... it had gone mad' (p. 83), as the postscript to his pamphlet ('Exterminate all the brutes') indicates. But it has destroyed him in turn, and he understands this when he exclaims 'The

horror! The horror'! (p. 86, see Theme on A Glimpsed Truth). Marlow also
has felt the power of the wilderness but above all he has felt its power over
Kurtz, with whom he struggles as with an *alter ego*. The difference between
the two men is that Marlow has exercised through his journey, and at the
climax of it, a restraint of which Kurtz has been incapable.

A GLIMPSED TRUTH

Marlow's first words in *Youth* are 'You fellows know there are those
voyages that seem ordered for the illustration of life, that might stand for a
symbol of existence'. *Heart of Darkness* deals with one such voyage and has
been called a 'poetic meditation on human existence'. The reader cannot
fail to be struck by Marlow's repeated self-questioning about the
behaviour of men, whether black or white, as well as about our position in
the universe and the meaning of life. These questions arise as a result of
Marlow's confrontation with 'the mystery of an unknown earth' (p. 19);
they are his reaction to a typically Conradian situation, that of the hero who
is cut off from family, friends and habitual social environment, and who is
tested in a crisis gone through in 'isolation' (p. 28), as is also the case in
Nostromo. One of his first discoveries as he travels away from his familiar
surroundings is an alteration of what can be termed 'real', and a sense of the
relativity of reality. On the African coast only the surf and the paddling
negroes give him a sense of 'reality' (p. 28), of something 'natural and true'
(p. 28). When he arrives at the Central Station, the whites and their
dealings seem to him increasingly 'unreal' (pp. 38 and 39) because he never
thought the white man was capable of such inefficiency, waste and
inhumanity. By contrast, he is impressed by the wilderness as 'something
great and invincible' (p. 38), by the mystery of the land and 'the amazing
reality of its concealed life' (p. 41). Marlow opposes two different views of
reality. One of them is linked with the value of work as an instrument of
self-discovery: 'I like what is in the work – the chance to find yourself. Your
own reality' (p. 44). This is largely synonymous with what he calls
elsewhere 'inborn strength' and 'deliberate belief' (p. 52) and it also
manifests itself in his capacity for restraint. These qualities are not the
white man's privilege, as Marlow himself insists when he presents the
cannibals as 'fine fellows … men one could work with' (p. 50), who also
show 'restraint' and 'inborn strength' (p. 58).

The other reality Marlow presents is embodied in the landscape. When he refers to 'the overwhelming realities of this strange world of plants, and water and silence' and adds 'It was the stillness of an implacable force brooding over an inscrutable intention' (p. 49), he seems to discern in the African landscape an indefinable presence, at once fascinating and threatening, 'an appeal or … a menace'. 'What was in there?' (p. 42) he asks. No final or clear answer is given to this question, and Marlow asserts that 'The inner truth is hidden – luckily, luckily' (p. 50). True, he had just described the appeal of the manager's uncle 'to the hidden evil' in the land. Does this mean, as is often suggested, that the reality at the heart of primitive nature is positively malignant? It seems rather that Marlow (or Joseph Conrad through him) presents untamed nature as the seat of a force that humans are too small to comprehend, and uses it as a reflector of that unknown part of our psyche which is itself the seat of contradictory impulses – as Kurtz illustrates. This may be part of Kurtz's 'glimpsed truth' (p. 87) and explains the 'commingling of desire and hate' (p. 87) in his final cry. As Marlow says, 'life is a greater riddle than some of us think it to be' (p. 87). What is certain is that the contrast between the reality of work, the capacity for achievement, which is something he understands, and the reality of the enigmatic living wilderness is at the centre of his vision of the world.

Even before formulating this antithesis of truth in the universe and man's 'own true stuff' (p. 52), Marlow asks another fundamental question: 'What were we who had strayed in here?' (p. 42). This is answered piecemeal in the course of the narrative. As already pointed out, humanity seems very small when confronted with a great and mysterious nature. While praising the saving virtue of efficiency, Marlow compares his progress on the river to that of a 'blindfolded man set to drive a van over a bad road' (p. 50). These can be read as images for a person's progress and performances in life. They suggest that, however seriously we take ourselves, we are like animals performing well but dangerously and for no clear purpose in a universe which we do not comprehend. It is as if the gods had wanted to play games with us, and, at the same time, it throws an ironic light on the white man's claim to infallibility and his view of himself as a 'supernatural being' (p. 66). In addition, Marlow states that what keeps the white man on the right path is the butcher, who saves him from the necessity of being a cannibal, and the policeman; that is, the institutions which civilised society sets up to ensure order. Without the support and check of these institutions we yield to our 'forgotten and brutal instincts' or to our 'monstrous passions' (p. 83), as Kurtz does, or like Decoud in *Nostromo* who gives in to despair and commits suicide.

It seems then that for Marlow (and Joseph Conrad) civilisation is a varnish which wears off as soon as we are cut off from the conditions that created it. Marlow's trip is also a return into 'the night of first ages' (p. 51). We can deduce from this that he views primitive peoples as the ancestors of so-called civilised peoples, an opinion confirmed by his response to the wilderness as to the past of man (pp. 51–2). Needless to say, this view is sharply criticised by African commentators who detect in it what they see as Joseph Conrad's racism. Admittedly, Marlow (and probably Joseph Conrad) shares some of the prejudices of his time and seems to adhere to a Eurocentric and Darwinian view of humanity. Yet he clearly suggests that the truth about humankind is not to be discovered in progress, nor obviously in the rationalism that prevailed in Europe since the Enlightenment. Truth appears when 'stripped of its cloak of time' (p. 52). He also insists that Africa and its inhabitants remain mysterious to him, an enigma. Together with Marlow's lie to the Intended, the truth which, Marlow says, Kurtz 'glimpsed' (p. 87) when he exclaimed 'The horror! The horror!' is the passage which has given rise to the most diverse interpretations: it is sometimes simply death; for some it is the horror of the 'Other' within oneself; the horror of 'going native'; conquest and its attendant evils; a condemnation by Kurtz of what he has done. If one keeps in mind the pride of Kurtz in his ideals and the eloquence with which he expresses them, one interpretation can certainly be that 'the horror' refers to his awareness of the discrepancy between those ideals and his utter failure to live up to them. The 'glimpsed truth' thus also points to the ineradicable duality of humankind and of our deeper instincts. As has been suggested, Kurtz's cry can equally be understood 'as a recoil from the whole mess of European rapacity and brutality in Africa into which he is being taken back' (Goonetilleke, p. 82). Therefore it is also a judgement on the failure of white civilisation.

One conclusion we can draw from these comments is that Joseph Conrad considerably widens the scope of fiction by presenting his actors not in society, as was usually the case in the nineteenth-century novel, but in a grandiose nature, giving Marlow's reflections a much deeper metaphysical dimension, while the multiple interpretations they continue to elicit are a sign of the novel's modernity. His presentation of a reality other than based on individual and social props was also new at the time. The ease with which a civilised person can discard the virtues that make for self-control and achievement in a situation of prolonged stress seems to have been the cause of Joseph Conrad's pessimism, even despair. These throw another light on Marlow's lie, which can also be explained as a refusal to question further the values of white civilisation. Joseph Conrad seems to have shared Winnie Verloc's opinion in *The Secret Agent* that 'things do not stand much looking into'.

NARRATIVE TECHNIQUE

THE STRUCTURE AND THE HANDLING OF TIME

One difficulty in analysing the text is that all its elements are interwoven and not easily separable. Several critics have rightly suggested that Joseph Conrad's narrative technique in *Heart of Darkness* is part of the meaning of the text, not just a means of conveying it. The beginning and the end of the novel, presented by a first narrator who introduces Marlow's tale and concludes on it, are usually referred to as the 'frame'. The presentation of a story within the story is a very modern device and has since led to a kind of novel in which a novelist or artist (and, as a narrator, Marlow is one) is the hero of his own work of art (see the reference to the *mise-en-abyme* in the first section). One major effect of Joseph Conrad's use of a frame and two narrators is to provoke a chain-like reaction: Marlow's story is told to four listeners, one of whom tells it to the readers, who may react differently to it as the listeners do. Among them are a lawyer, an accountant, the company director. Note that their profession makes them participants in the imperialist venture and that they serve its interests like the company director and the accountant Marlow meets in Brussels and in Africa. The unnamed first narrator is the only one who takes part imaginatively in Marlow's tale and is changed by it too, as his awareness at the end of the story that the Thames leads 'into the heart of an immense darkness' (p. 95) indicates. During one of Marlow's major interruptions he says 'I listened, I listened on the watch for the sentence, for the word, that would give me the clue to the faint uneasiness inspired by this narrative' (p. 43). His uneasiness, like Marlow's, is an incentive to *seeing* and understanding the moral significance of Marlow's experience. The other listeners, on the contrary, either sleep through Marlow's tale and thus remain unaware, or do not see what he is driving at, as can be inferred from their reactions (pp. 50 and 63).

The contrast between this unawareness and Marlow's attempt to understand highlights the significance of the frame. In spite of the brooding gloom over London, the first narrator uses expressions like 'serenity', 'exquisite brilliance', 'pacifically', 'benign', 'unstained light' (p. 18) to describe the end of the day. The optimistic view of colonialism he expresses afterwards matches his view of the landscape. When Marlow says 'And this also ... has been one of the dark places of the earth' (p. 19), the effect is the more striking and supposes a deeper, imaginative response to his surroundings. So are his comments on the individual's participation in a colonialist expedition: 'imagine the growing regrets, the longing to escape, the powerless disgust, the surrender, the hate' (p. 21), words which naturally prefigure Kurtz's predicament. As a matter of fact, the first narrator's introduction raises central issues developed by Marlow's narrative: the dark role of the city as a centre of 'civilization', the nature of colonialism, the individual's capacity to reflect on it and to explore his or her own mind.

The division of the narrative into three chapters seems, at first, arbitrary. Each break, however, occurs at a significant moment in Marlow's approach to Kurtz: the first break when he has only heard of him and wonders whether Kurtz is equal to the moral ideas he propounds; the second at the height of Marlow's curiosity about Kurtz just before he discovers what he is really like. Similarly, each pause in the narrative has a specific function and draws attention to Marlow's listeners and their reactions. The first substantial interruption (p. 21), for example, elicits from the first narrator his comment on the inconclusiveness of Marlow's experience and awakens the reader's curiosity about the nature of Marlow's tale and therefore of the novel. Another significant pause takes place when one listener has apparently broken it with the exclamation: 'Absurd!' (p. 63). Lawrence Graver writes that this interruption so unnerves Marlow that it leads to a five-page outburst in which he summarises nearly every major theme in the story (Graver, *Conrad's Short Fiction*, 1979, p. 79). Certainly, Marlow sounds emotionally involved, as if he had not wholly digested his experience, when he anticipates his meeting with Kurtz and focuses his attention on the kind of temptation with which Kurtz was confronted (see pp. 63–7).

While making the reader aware of the effect Kurtz has on Marlow, this passage further delays his account of the actual meeting with Kurtz and, like Marlow's other anticipations or **flashforwards**, adds to the suspense he gradually builds up, while making it clear that meeting Kurtz is his ultimate goal. At the same time, Marlow's several allusions to Kurtz before his actual appearance in the tale show that Marlow himself proceeds through an association of ideas rather than strictly chronologically. Thanks to this method we know all about Kurtz before Marlow relates their meeting; when this takes place, he can concentrate on his struggle with him.

Edward Said writes that Joseph Conrad uses a 'retrospective method' (*Joseph Conrad and the Fiction of Autobiography*, 1966, p. viii) which allows him to interpret what he could not reflect on at the time of experience (p. 88), though one must also point out that Marlow (Joseph Conrad's mediator) asks himself as many questions as he gives answers in his interpretation. In the course of the narrative Marlow moves backward and forward in time, thus introducing the past into the present of the narration and indirectly showing how important the past is to understand the present and how interrelated past, present and future are. For example, he alludes to the past (the timeless and primeval world he explores), then to the future (Kurtz, but also the possible development of any person's mind) and thus illustrates his own assertion that 'the mind of man is capable of anything' (p. 52). The timeshifts in his comments figure as important clues in his own experience and in his attempt to convey it to his listeners. In Part I, for instance, Marlow interrupts the account of his conversation with the brickmaker to question himself about the mystery of the landscape, then about Kurtz whom he hasn't yet met. Addressing his listeners, he asks 'Do you see him [Kurtz]? Do you see the story? Do you see anything?' (p. 42). To make the reader *see* is the artist's purpose as defined by Joseph Conrad in his preface to *The Nigger of the Narcissus*.

Marlow's questions at this stage emphasise the difficulty of making clear the nature of his experience. But in Part II he overhears, in a conversation between the Manager and his uncle, that Kurtz on his way back to the Central Station suddenly decided, after travelling three hundred miles, to turn back and return alone to the Inner Station. Marlow's comment is 'I seemed to *see* Kurtz for the first time. It was a distinct glimpse' (p. 47, italics mine). The glimpse, as we realise later, when he alludes to his actual meeting with Kurtz (pp. 63–7), is what attracts Kurtz to the 'savagery' of the Inner Station, a glimpse also of his dual nature and of the contradiction between his eloquence and the destructiveness expressed in the postscript to his report (p. 66). It seems then that Marlow's disruptions of the chronology of his tale are part of the 'haze' or 'misty halo' which contribute to its meaning but are not concentrated in its centre 'like a kernel' (p. 20).

Irony

Irony is one of Joseph Conrad's favourite methods in this as in other novels. It is a device by which a writer expresses a meaning which contradicts the stated or ostensible one. Its effect in *Heart of Darkness* is to intensify Marlow's indignation and render it more effectively than if he expressed it in so many words. It also provokes in the reader the same reaction as in Marlow. There are several ways of achieving irony. One of them is called 'verbal irony' and occurs when the real meaning of the words is the opposite of that which is literally expressed. Marlow has frequent recourse to it. Referring to the hens over which Fresleven fought and, as a result, was killed, he says 'the cause of progress got them' and calls the affair 'glorious' (p. 24), emphasising the futility of the reason for which Fresleven died. He brings out the little seriousness with which some European nations take their colonising mission by calling colonialists on the East Coast of Africa 'the jolly pioneers of progress' (p. 24). Marlow's salutation *'Ave! … Morituri te salutant'* (p. 25) points to the discrepancy between the grandiloquent expression and the actual meanness of the enterprise in which he takes part.

Calling colonialism 'the merry dance of death and trade' (p. 29) or 'high and just proceedings' (p. 31); exclaiming 'the work!' (p. 32) while meditating over 'the great demoralisation of the land' (p. 33), these are so many examples of a contemptuous and incisive verbal irony. Perhaps less obvious but just as effective is the ironic contrast between the colonialists' professions of intention and what they are actually up to; the masterstroke of this kind of irony lies in the contrast between Kurtz's eloquence and the postscript to his report: 'Exterminate all the brutes!' (p. 66).

This example is less one of verbal than of dramatic irony, which is conveyed through the structure of a work of art. In the Author's Note to the original edition of the novel Joseph Conrad wrote that his 'sombre theme had to be given a sinister resonance ... a continued vibration that ... would hang in the air and dwell on the ear after the last note had been struck'. He succeeds in doing so through the pervasive irony of Marlow's narrative, conveyed through a series of parallels, contrasts and echoes. To the first narrator, for example, the Thames has the 'dignity of a waterway leading to the uttermost ends of the earth' (p. 18) but Marlow points out that England too was once 'the end of the world' (p. 20). Though not immediately obvious, another parallel is provided between Roman, British and Belgian imperialism since all are 'hunters for gold', robbers or buccaneers. This parallel is clearly part of Joseph Conrad's ironic intention reinforced by Marlow's remark that 'none of us would feel exactly like this' (p. 21), a remark belied by his tale. There is an ironic contrast between the darkness at the 'grove of death' and the brightness of the accountant's outfit, between the hardly bearable atmosphere and his saying that he came out 'to get a breath of fresh air' (p. 33), between the fact that his books are 'in apple-pie order' while 'Everything else in the station was in a muddle – heads, things, buildings' (p. 33). The juxtaposition of 'heads' and 'things' is ironical too. The same kind of ironic contrast is afforded by the efficiency inherent in the old book on seamanship and the utter uselessness of such a book to the harlequin in the jungle. One kind of pervasive irony grows out of the repeated opposition between the littleness of man and the powerful greatness of the landscape. The whisper of Kurtz's last cry echoes through the end of the novel but does so most ironically when Marlow hears it together with the Intended's self-deceived idealistic comments. Joseph Conrad's use of parallels and contrasts might be called an associative method. It relies for effect not on explicit statement but, as in poetry, on the reader's capacity to trace these associations. As we shall see, Joseph Conrad's ironic method also applies to his use of symbolism and imagery.

SYMBOLISM AND IMAGERY

While *Heart of Darkness* was being serialized Joseph Conrad wrote about it 'I don't start with an abstract notion. I start with definite images'. He was so much aware of the poetic elements in *Heart of Darkness* that at one stage he was experimenting with his narrative and scanning it into blank verse. It could be demonstrated that this novel is poetic in its very conception and that practically every element in its literary structure contributes to its symbolism.

The title is symbolic and covers a psychological as much as a geographical reality. It refers to the ambivalent force at the heart of the wilderness; it also stands for the central darkness Kurtz discovers within himself, and possibly at the heart of all civilised consciousness. The title indirectly alludes to the setting, which is also symbolic. The use of Africa as an inner, unknown, territory was not new. As early a writer as Sir Thomas Browne (1605–82) wrote in *Religio Medici* (1642): 'We carry within us the wonders we seek without us: there is all Africa and her prodigies in us'. Saul Bellow (b.1915), a contemporary American writer, wrote in *Henderson the Rain King* (1959): 'Well, maybe every guy has his own Africa'. The plot of *Heart of Darkness*, the voyage from Outer to Central to Inner Station, symbolises a journey into the self. If we think of Marlow's voice reaching his listeners in the growing darkness from the depths of his consciousness the very telling of the tale becomes symbolic of an inner voyage. The actual journey offers more through a second level of interpretation. Critics have read in it a descent into humankind's unconscious (see Themes) or into an underworld recalling similar episodes to those of the *Aeneid*, an epic poem by Virgil (70–19BC) or the *Divine Comedy* by Dante (1265–1321), or in the Orpheus legend. It has also been suggested that Marlow's journey stands for the quest of the grail originally told in medieval legends. This interpretation would naturally apply to Marlow's quest of Kurtz, not to the manager's agents. Indeed, when Marlow uses words with a religious connotation such as 'pilgrims', 'god' or 'pray', he is strongly ironical and merely implies that the manager and his followers have deified their commercial interests.

The characters, too, are symbolic. Kurtz can be looked upon as Marlow's shadow, and when Marlow first meets him, he seems to be coming up from the ground (p. 75). The natives at the 'grove of death' are like phantoms in hell. The native mistress represents the African soul while the Intended stands for the idealism of Western civilisation. The painting by Kurtz in the brickmaker's hut 'representing a woman, draped and blindfolded, carrying a lighted torch' (p. 40) seems to symbolise both the

'idea' and the Intended. It is strongly ironical since, in spite of the torch she
carries, the woman cannot see. Other objects Marlow comes across carry a
symbolic meaning: the derelict machinery at the Outer Station points to
the destructive impact of Africa on what has been created by white
civilisation. Most impressive, however, is the symbolism of the landscape
descriptions. To take but one example, Marlow describes the effect of the
jungle on him one night at the Central Station:

> The great wall of vegetation, an exuberant and entangled mass of trunks, branches,
> leaves, boughs, festoons, motionless in the moonlight, was like a rioting invasion of
> soundless life, a rolling wave of plants, piled up, crested, ready to topple over the
> creek, to sweep every little man of us out of his little existence. (p. 45)

Apart from its fusion of immobility and movement, Joseph Conrad's use of
a sea image ('a rolling wave … crested … ready to topple') conveys the
sense of threatening engulfment Marlow experiences and foreshadows the
impact of the jungle on Kurtz. Taken together, however, Joseph Conrad's
poetic descriptions of the African interior create a dense and populated
inner landscape at the heart of every person's consciousness.

The 'light and darkness' imagery pervades the narrative and is one of
Joseph Conrad's most effective tools in conveying his meaning.
Conventional symbolism associates light and white with good, black with
evil. Joseph Conrad mostly departs from this connotation, and even when
he adheres to it, he does so in a subtle and complex way. At the beginning
of the novel light shines on the Thames estuary, whereas a brooding gloom
envelops London. The brooding gloom is mentioned five times in three
pages. It is the more ironic as London, 'the greatest town on earth' (p. 17),
is the greatest centre of progress and that it is from here that 'bearers of a
spark from the sacred fire' of civilisation (p. 19) start. In the Author's Note
to *The Secret Agent* Joseph Conrad calls London 'a cruel devourer of the
world's light'. At the beginning of *Heart of Darkness* the sun over the estuary
is 'striken to death' (p. 18) by the touch of the gloom over the city, a
powerful image suggesting that people are responsible for the darkness in
the world. The phrase 'a brooding gloom in sunshine' (p. 19) sums up the
theme of the novel, the existence of darkness at the core of a shining
civilisation; it is echoed by a similar image at the Inner Station: 'All this
[Kurtz's hut and the heads on poles] was in the gloom, while we down there
were yet in the sunshine' (p. 75). The sunlight at the Outer Station is

'blinding' (p. 30), and the accountant is a blind man indeed. Here all that is associated with light and the white man, the symbolic piece of white worsted around the neck of a dying slave, the accountant's shining outfit, is a source of appalling darkness and suggests a complete reversal of values. The torch-light on Kurtz's painting has a sinister effect. The postscript to Kurtz's report is 'luminous and terrifying, like a flash of lightning in a serene sky' (p. 66) and blazes with a light of destruction. Most ironic of all is the association of light and darkness during Marlow's interview with the Intended. The windows in the room, normally a source of light, are 'luminous and bedraped columns' (p. 91) as in a mortuary. The 'cold and monumental whiteness' of the fireplace adds to the deathlike atmosphere. While the Intended talks, her forehead 'illumined by the unextinguishable light of belief and love' (p. 92), the darkness in the room deepens as if to contradict her words, and this recalls the ambivalence of Kurtz's gift of eloquence: 'the pulsating stream of light, or the deceitful flow from the heart of an impenetrable darkness' (p. 63).

Images of death also abound in the novel, linking the white men's activities in the metropolis with their actions in the wilderness. Brussels is twice compared to a sepulchre (pp. 24 and 88). The company headquarters are like 'a house in a city of the dead' (p. 26). The Intended's house is in a street like 'a well-kept alley in a cemetery' (p. 90), and the piano in her drawingroom is like a 'sarcophagus' (p. 91). These images intimate that she too is at the source of the deadly enterprise. Both blacks and whites are its victims. We can visualise the 'massacre' of blacks reduced to 'phantoms' at the 'grove of death' but Kurtz, himself 'an animated image of death' (p. 76), is both its agent and its victim. The comparison of the accountant to a 'hair-dresser's dummy' (p. 33) and of the brickmaker's eyes to 'mica discs' (p. 40) express death through dehumanisation. So does the transformation of men into 'raw matter' (p. 30). The pilgrims' greed for ivory generates death: 'A taint of imbecile rapacity blew through it all, like a whiff from some corpse' (p. 38). The association between ivory and death is even clearer in the macabre juxtaposition that suggests itself between the 'ivory ball' (p. 64) of Kurtz's head and the 'black, dried, sunken' (p. 74) ball of the head on the pole. There are other images less obviously connected with death but equally suggestive of the destructive or futile presence of the white man in Africa. The hole is one of them. There is the purposeless 'vast artificial hole' (p. 31) at the 'grove of death', the hole in the pail the pilgrim uses to stop the fire at the Central Station; the manager has made a hole in the bottom of the steamer on some rocks, thus delaying the rescue of Kurtz and possibly hastening his death. The growing grass invading the remains of men and of their achievements is another recurring image, an ironic comment on the evanescence of human existence.

LANGUAGE AND STYLE

In 'Conrad: the Presentation of Narrative', Edward Said rightly points out that Joseph Conrad's 'Narratives originate in the hearing and telling presence of people' (Said, *The World, the Text and the Critic*, 1984, p. 95). This is a way of emphasising the 'orality' of his tales. It is particularly true of *Heart of Darkness*, in which at some stage both Marlow and Kurtz are perceived as disembodied voices. This technique explains to some extent the hesitancy in Marlow's narrative, the difficulty he often alludes to of making his hearers perceive what he is trying to convey as well as the difficulty of finding the right words to convey it. It also helps to bring out the disparity one senses in Marlow's tale between his efforts to convey the real nature of his experience and the language at his disposal to do so.

The parallels and contrasts in the narrative, its symbolism and imagery, are aspects of style – the unique or specific verbal pattern a writer uses to express his meaning. Joseph Conrad's style in *Heart of Darkness* is marked by repetitions which have a cumulative effect and also contribute to the 'vibration' which, so he hoped, would still impress the reader after closing the book. Another musical characteristic of his writing is his frequent use of alliteration as in the 'slimy swell swung' (p. 29). He sometimes creates a weird effect by giving a voice to the landscape itself only referring implicitly to the people in it as in 'the mist itself had screamed' (p. 55), 'the bush began to howl' (p. 61) or 'a weird incantation came out of the black, flat wall of the woods' (p. 80). (See also Text 2 of Textual Analysis.)

George Orwell (1903–50), in his novel *1984* (1949), shows how language can be corrupted for political purposes. Long before him, Joseph Conrad showed the same in *Heart of Darkness*. See, for example, the way in which the exploited natives are called 'criminals', 'enemies' and 'rebels'. There is also black humour in the novel, as when Marlow calls the pilgrims 'unwholesome' and 'unappetising'. One objection sometimes jars with the chorus of approval of Joseph Conrad's style: it bears on his frequent use of adjectives such as 'impenetrable', 'inconceivable' or 'inscrutable'. F.R. Leavis wrote that Joseph Conrad 'is intent on making a virtue out of not knowing what he means' (Leavis, *The Great Tradition*, 1962, p. 199). Several arguments have been used to counter this opinion. Generally, they are to the effect that Marlow does mean to convey his bewilderment in the face of the mysteriousness of what he describes and to draw attention to its inexpressibility. Joseph Conrad himself claimed 'an inalienable right to the use of all my epithets', a proof, if necessary, that they are part of his artistic purpose.

PART FOUR

TEXTUAL ANALYSIS

TEXT 1   (PAGES 20–1)

'I was thinking of very old times, when the Romans first came here, nineteen
hundred years ago – the other day .... Light came out of this river since – you say
Knights? Yes; but it is like a running blaze on a plain, like a flash of lightning in the
clouds. We live in the flicker – may it last as long as the old earth keeps rolling! But
darkness was here yesterday. Imagine the feelings of a commander of fine – what
d'ye call 'em? – trireme in the Mediterranean, ordered suddenly to the north; run
overland across the Gauls in a hurry; put in charge of one of these craft the
legionaries – a wonderful lot of handy men they must have been too – used to build,
apparently by the hundred, in a month or two, if we may believe what we read.
Imagine him here – the very end of the world, a sea the colour of lead, a sky the
colour of smoke, a kind of ship about as rigid as a concertina – and going up this
river with stores, or orders, or what you like. Sandbanks, marshes, forests, savages –
precious little to eat fit for a civilised man, nothing but Thames water to drink.
No Falernian wine here, no going ashore. Here and there a military camp lost in a
wilderness, like a needle in a bundle of hay – cold, fog, tempests, disease, exile, and
death – death skulking in the air, in the water, in the bush. They must have been
dying like flies here. Oh yes – he did it. Did it very well, too, no doubt, and without
thinking much about it either, except afterwards to brag of what he had gone
through in his time, perhaps. They were men enough to face the darkness. And
perhaps he was cheered by keeping his eye on a chance of promotion to the fleet at
Ravenna by and by, if he had good friends in Rome and survived the awful climate.
Or think of a decent young citizen in a toga – perhaps too much dice, you know –
coming out here in the train of some prefect, or tax-gatherer, or trader, even, to
mend his fortunes. Land in a swamp, march through the woods, and in some inland
post feel the savagery, the utter savagery, had closed round him – all that mysterious
life of the wilderness that stirs in the forest, in the jungles, in the hearts of wild men.
There's no initiation either into such mysteries. He has to live in the midst of the
incomprehensible, which is also detestable. And it has a fascination, too, that goes to
work upon him. The fascination of the abomination – you know. Imagine the
growing regrets, the longing to escape, the powerless disgust, the surrender, the
hate.'

He paused.

'Mind,' he began again, lifting one arm from the elbow, the palm of the hand outwards, so that, with his legs folded before him, he had the pause of a Buddha preaching in European clothes and without a lotus-flower – 'Mind, none of us would feel exactly like this. What saves us is efficiency – the devotion to efficiency. But these chaps were not much account, really. They were no colonists; their administration was merely a squeeze, and nothing more, I suspect. They were conquerors, and for that you want only brute force – nothing to boast of, when you have it, since your strength is just an accident arising from the weakness of others. They grabbed what they could get for the sake of what was to be got. It was just robbery with violence, aggravated murder on a great scale, and men going at it blind – as is very proper for those who tackle a darkness. The conquest of the earth, which mostly means the taking it away from those who have a different complexion or slightly flatter noses than ourselves, is not a pretty thing when you look into it too much. What redeems it is the idea only. An idea at the back of it; not a sentimental pretence but an idea; and an unselfish belief in the idea – something you can set up, and bow down before, and offer a sacrifice to ....'

It has been suggested already that the novel's first episode, from which this extract is quoted, presents in a nutshell the development of the whole narrative. In the passage quoted above the theme of imperialism is clearly illustrated by Marlow's evocation of the Roman invasion of Britain and by his general comment on 'the conquest of the earth'. So are the metaphysical reflections and questioning that Marlow is prone to while telling his story ('we live in the flicker'). Moreover, when he alludes to the 'growing regrets, the longing to escape, the powerless disgust, the surrender, the hate' experienced by the Roman invaders, he implies that, in some measure at least, they were aware of the nature of their expedition and that for them, as later for Kurtz, it was a journey into the self.

The parallel between ancient and modern imperialism is expressed through a striking and ironic juxtaposition. The Romans came to Britain 'nineteen hundred years ago' but this was only 'the other day' or 'yesterday', which suggests not only the relativity of time but, together with the 'flash of lightning in the clouds' and 'we live in the flicker' conveys the brevity of human existence when compared to that of the universe. It recalls the insignificance of men as expressed by Shakespeare in *King Lear* where they are compared to flies, as Marlow also does later in the passage. Moreover, the bringing together of Roman and modern imperialism implies that humanity has not progressed, the two periods showing men behaving in a similar way. The Romans were indeed men 'used to build', like modern empire-builders. As individuals 'going up this river' (the Thames – p. 20), they were clearly as alienated as Marlow and his companions 'going up that river' (the Congo – p. 49) when travelling towards the darkness, being aware only of 'marshes, forests, savages'. Nor could they go ashore, exactly like Marlow. They had friends in the metropolis who could put in a good word for them and help them in their career, again like the colonists in the Congo. Marlow even alludes to the Romans who came to Britain to 'mend [their] fortunes' like his companion on the way to the Central Station who came only to the Congo 'to make money'.

The words Marlow uses in this early part of his tale, 'the mysterious life of the wilderness that stirs in the forest, in the jungles, in the heart of wild men' foreshadow similar descriptions of Marlow's experience in the Congo and throw an ironic light on British civilisation since this was only 'the other day'. All these are examples of Joseph Conrad's associative method and of the underlying, though possibly unconscious, irony of Marlow's narrative technique.

The last paragraph in the passage prefigures Marlow's (and at a further remove Joseph Conrad's) ambivalent and even ambiguous presentation of imperialism. When he says that the Romans were no 'colonists', he asserts indirectly that real colonisers are aware of their civilising mission whereas 'conquerors' are mere robbers and murderers. However, from his general critical statement on the 'conquest of the earth' we may assume that no conquest (a prerequisite to colonialism) is immune from such evils. Yet he also asserts that the conquest of other people's territories is redeemed by the idea (an assertion clearly belied later by Kurtz's experience, though preserved as a 'saving illusion' for his Intended), while the individuals who take part in such ventures ('us') are saved by efficiency. This proves true at least in Marlow's case.

TEXT 2   (PAGES 54–6)

'Towards the evening of the second day we judged ourselves about eight miles from Kurtz's station. I wanted to push on; but the manager looked grave, and told me the navigation up there was so dangerous that it would be advisable, the sun being very low already, to wait where we were till next morning. Moreover, he pointed out that if the warning to approach cautiously were to be followed, we must approach in daylight – not at dusk, or in the dark. This was sensible enough. Eight miles meant nearly three hours' steaming for us, and I could also see suspicious ripples at the upper end of the reach. Nevertheless, I was annoyed beyond expression at the delay, and most unreasonably too, since one more night could not matter much after so many months. As we had plenty of wood, and caution was the word, I brought up in the middle of the stream. The reach was narrow, straight, with high sides like a railway cutting. The dusk came gliding into it long before the sun had set. The current ran smooth and swift, but a dumb immobility sat on the banks. The living trees, lashed together by the creepers and every living bush of the undergrowth, might have been changed into stone, even to the slenderest twig, to the lightest leaf. It was not sleep – it seemed unnatural, like a state of trance. Not the faintest sound of any kind could be heard. You looked on amazed, and began to suspect yourself of being deaf – then the night came suddenly, and struck you blind as well. About three in the morning some large fish leaped, and the loud splash made me jump as though a gun had been fired. When the sun rose there was a white fog, very warm and clammy, and more blinding than the night. It did not shift or drive; it was just there, standing all round you like something solid. At eight or nine, perhaps, it lifted as a shutter lifts. We had a glimpse of the towering multitude of trees, of the immense matted jungle, with the blazing little ball of the sun hanging over it – all perfectly still – and then the white shutter came down again, smoothly, as if sliding in greased grooves. I ordered the chain, which we had begun to heave in, to be paid out again. Before it stopped running with a muffled rattle, a cry, a very loud cry, as of infinite desolation, soared slowly in the opaque air. It ceased. A complaining clamour, modulated in savage discords, filled our ears. The sheer unexpectedness of it made my hair stir under my cap. I don't know how it struck the others: to me it seemed as though the mist itself had screamed, so suddenly, and apparently from all sides at once, did this tumultuous and mournful uproar arise. It culminated in a hurried outbreak of almost intolerably excessive shrieking, which stopped short, leaving us stiffened in a variety of silly attitudes, and obstinately listening to the nearly as appalling and excessive silence. "Good God! What is the meaning –?" stammered at my elbow one of the pilgrims – a little fat man, with sandy hair and red whiskers, who wore side-spring boots, and pink pyjamas tucked into his socks. Two others remained open-mouthed a whole minute, then dashed into the little cabin, to rush out incontinently and stand darting scared glances, with Winchesters at "ready" in their hands. What we could see was just the steamer we were on, her outlines blurred as though she had been on the point of dissolving, and a misty strip of water, perhaps two feet broad, around her – and that was all. The rest of the world was nowhere, as far as our eyes and ears were concerned. Just nowhere. Gone, disappeared; swept off without leaving a whisper or a shadow behind.'

Marlow, the manager and some pilgrims are now on their way to the Inner Station. To Marlow's great annoyance the manager further delays their progress towards Kurtz, though Marlow must acknowledge that it might be dangerous to proceed further in the dusk. This obstacle in time is paralleled with one in space as the fog which envelops them renders more difficult their approach to the geographical and psychological Inner Station.

The interesting passage in this extract starts with a description of the utter immobility of the forest on both sides of the river. The '*living* trees' and the '*living* bush' even to the '*slenderest* twig, to the *lightest* leaf' seem to have been turned into *stone* (italics mine). *Living* nature, then, appears to have become utterly inanimate like stone, and this actually reflects what might be called the deadness of the white men approaching the Inner Station. Indeed in the next sentence the utter silence of the bush and the darkness of the night make Marlow suspect that they are deaf and blind. In other words, the state of nature has a direct effect on the men, depriving them of their senses (hearing and seeing), though one can also say that nature gives concrete form to the *white* man's incapacity (suggested in '*white* fog') to perceive and understand the kind of reality he is approaching, and this is confirmed when in the morning the white fog is 'more *blinding* than the night' (italics mine). When at the end of the passage Marlow says that 'the rest of the world was nowhere as far as our eyes and ears were concerned', they seem to have lost the support of the real concrete world altogether and to confront what Marlow later calls an 'unfathomable enigma and a mystery' (p. 58), which arouses in the pilgrims bewilderment and fear, as their nervous reactions show.

In the meantime, however, a cry of 'infinite desolation' has broken through 'the opaque air' and, as Marlow says, 'it seemed as though the mist itself had screamed' (p. 55). Not only is nature humanised by this cry, it is brought back to life by the sorrow ('desolation', 'mournful uproar'), the 'desperate grief' (p. 58) of Kurtz's African friends. This suggests that landscape itself is not passive but expresses a variety of emotions and moods, not necessarily as a mere projection of our own feelings (as, for example, in some Romantic poetry), but because of its own livingness, which, as Wilson Harris points out, disrupts the fixed (stony) prejudices of the whites towards Africa (in Hamner, *Joseph Conrad*, 1990, p.166).

A close attention to Joseph Conrad's use of nouns and adjectives in this passage should help the reader understand how Joseph Conrad's language endows both the men and nature with similar characteristics and how symbolism functions in the narrative. Here by an ironic reversal of the symbolism of the colour white, usually associated with light, it stands for darkness and blindness rather than enlightenment.

TEXT 3   (PAGES 87–8)

'However, as you see, I did not go to join Kurtz there and then. I did not. I remained to dream the nightmare out to the end, and to show my loyalty to Kurtz once more. Destiny. My destiny! Droll thing life is – that mysterious arrangement of merciless logic for a futile purpose. The most you can hope from it is some knowledge of yourself – that comes too late – a crop of unextinguishable regrets. I have wrestled with death. It is the most unexciting contest you can imagine. It takes place in an impalpable greyness, with nothing underfoot, with nothing around, without spectators, without clamour, without glory, without the great desire of victory, without the great fear of defeat, in a sickly atmosphere of tepid scepticism, without much belief in your own right, and still less in that of your adversary. If such is the form of ultimate wisdom, then life is a greater riddle than some of us think it to be. I was within a hair's-breath of the last opportunity for pronouncement, and I found with humiliation that probably I would have nothing to say. This is the reason why I affirm that Kurtz was a remarkable man. He had something to say. He said it. Since I had peeped over the edge myself, I understand better the meaning of his stare, that could not see the flame of the candle, but was wide enough to embrace the whole universe, piercing enough to penetrate all the hearts that beat in the darkness. He had summed up – he had judged. "The horror!" He was a remarkable man. After all, this was the expression of some sort of belief; it had candour, it had conviction, it had a vibrating note of revolt in its whisper, it had the appalling face of a glimpsed truth – the strange commingling of desire and hate. And it is not my own extremity I remember best – a vision of greyness without form filled with physical pain, and a careless contempt for the evanescence of all things – even of this pain itself. No! It is his extremity that I seem to have lived through. True, he had made that last stride, he had stepped over the edge, while I had been permitted to draw back my hesitating foot. And perhaps in this is the whole difference; perhaps all the wisdom, and all truth, and all sincerity, are just compressed into that inappreciable moment of time in which we step over the threshold of the invisible. Perhaps! I like to think my summing-up would not have been a word of careless contempt. Better his cry – much better. It was an affirmation, a moral victory paid for by innumerable defeats, by abominable terrors, by abominable satisfactions. But it was a victory! That is why I have remained loyal to Kurtz to the last, and even beyond, when a long time after I heard once more, not his own voice, but the echo of his magnificent eloquence thrown to me from a soul as translucently pure as a cliff of crystal.'

This passage offers another philosophical meditation, in which Marlow compares his own reaction to menacing death to Kurtz's moment of truth just before he died. Marlow intimates that the way we die depends on the way we have lived and that the meaning of death grows out of the significance of life or at least of our understanding of what we made of it. This does not prevent him from being very pessimistic about life, whose purpose, he says, is futile while our understanding of what we are comes too late for us to amend our ways, as is clearly the case with Kurtz. The evocation of his own (Marlow's) struggle with death is utterly unheroic: 'nothing underfoot … nothing around … without clamour, without glory', implies that people face death alone as they face life alone ('we live as we dream … alone'), without any support, as when Marlow and his companions were stopped by the fog (see Text 2). The dullness of that struggle, the lingering uncertainty and scepticism about the meaning of life and a possible afterlife are poles apart from the wisdom usually attributed to the dying person in more positive or more conventional perceptions of life and death. Marlow's feeling that he would have had nothing to say if he had actually stepped 'over the threshold of the invisible' may be a modest acknowledgement of his lack of achievement. But together with his earlier comment on the futility of life, it points to its meaninglessness and explains why so many critics emphasise Joseph Conrad's nihilism and despair.

In Marlow's eyes Kurtz's 'glimpsed truth', whatever it stands for (see Themes), is a moral victory because he has achieved 'some knowledge of [himself]'; he dies with an apparently full consciousness both of his own role in life and possibly of what death has in store for him and for humanity generally. Consciousness then is all important to Marlow and at a further remove to Joseph Conrad. Both are in a sense 'vessels' through which Kurtz's experience can be re-lived and re-created ('It is his extremity that I seem to have lived through'). It is as if Marlow's (and Joseph Conrad's) imagination had to go through such an ordeal in order to be able to tell a story in which so many facets of human experience coalesce: the possessiveness enacted in the acquisition of territories, of people, of material riches; the initiation that accompanies expeditions of conquest; and the many questions concerning the meaning of existence which arise when one is faced with the unknown.

At the end of the passage Marlow asserts that Kurtz's 'moral victory' justifies his own subsequent lie to the Intended. Calling her 'a soul as translucently pure as a cliff of crystal' becomes ironic in retrospect since her purity rests on ignorance and self-deception. Marlow's opinion that women should be kept in that ignorance is both a homage, since they keep the 'idea' alive, and a derogatory comment because women are 'out of touch with truth' (p. 27) and incapable of facing it. This view is now sharply criticised by feminist critics.

PART FIVE

BACKGROUND

JOSEPH CONRAD

Joseph Conrad has a unique position in English letters: he wrote in a language that was not native to him, and his novels have little in common with the comedy of manners that was fashionable when he began to write. His real name was Joseph Teodor Konrad Nalecz Korzeniowski. He was born on 3 December 1857 in a part of Poland that was under Russian domination. His parents were ardent patriots who belonged to the Polish landed gentry and bitterly resented the partition of their country between Russia, Germany and Austria. His father, who had a chivalrous and romantic temperament, injudiciously took part in a revolution that failed. He was arrested and exiled to the north of Moscow. His wife insisted on sharing his exile, with their little boy; she died of the hardship they endured when Joseph Conrad was seven. His father's health also failed and he died after their return to Poland, when Joseph Conrad was eleven. Joseph Conrad seems to have remembered from his father's personality the qualities of duty, courage and fidelity which he so much admired and which are later to be found in some of the characters in his novels.

After his parents' death Joseph Conrad was placed under the care of his maternal uncle, Thaddeus Bobrowski. As a Polish aristocrat, Joseph Conrad's cultural background was Western and he spoke and read considerably in French. But his father, himself a poet and a dramatist, had been an admirer of English literature, and so as a child Joseph Conrad read Shakespeare and Dickens in translation. When he lived alone with his father he was always reading or day-dreaming and developed a passion for travel and adventure. He did not take to the formal schooling he received after his father's death, and as early as 1872 began to beg his uncle to be allowed to go to sea. He was finally given permission to do so when he was seventeen, although his family resented his becoming an ordinary sailor and his apparent rejection of his cultural and social background. He left Poland for Marseilles and for four years led an adventurous life – not only at sea. On his second voyage he seems to have been involved in illegal activities in a Latin-American country, and this later provided material for his great novel *Nostromo* (1904). In Marseilles he helped to smuggle guns to the Spanish Carlists (the supporters of Don Carlos VII) and had a love affair with a beautiful Basque adventuress, which ended with his attempted suicide. These experiences were later recalled in his novel *The Arrow of Gold* (1919).

Much has been made of Joseph Conrad's subsequent transfer from the French to the British merchant navy, because it led eventually to his becoming an English novelist. He was twenty-one when he first came to England and knew very little English then. He taught himself the language, and spent the next fifteen to twenty years at sea, rising from the lowest rank to become a captain. He travelled frequently to the Far East (where many of his stories are set) as well as to India and Australia. In 1886 he became a British citizen.

Although Joseph Conrad acknowledged his debt to the French writer Maupassant (1850–93), he was exasperated by the rumour that he had hesitated between French and English when he started writing. He made a point of refuting this story, writing: 'English was for me neither a matter of choice nor adoption ... there was adoption; but it was I who was adopted by the genius of the language ... its very idioms ... had a direct action on my temperament and fashioned my still plastic character'. Although his first published novel, *Almayer's Folly*, was not published until 1895, it seems that Joseph Conrad tried his hand at writing stories as early as 1886. The 'tales of hearsay' that all sailors tell helped to shape his technique as a novelist, though from the first Joseph Conrad was less interested in events as such than in their impact on characters and in the view of reality they revealed. In 1890 he went to the Belgian Congo, as a result of which his health was permanently impaired. This contributed to his giving up the sea a few years later, a decision confirmed by his marriage in 1896 to an English girl sixteen years younger than himself. His marriage was a happy one; his wife was good-natured and competent and provided the emotional stability he needed. He died of a heart attack in 1924 while writing a novel about Napoleon's return from Elba.

There is a sense in which *Heart of Darkness* is a 'Personal Record' for the autobiographical element in it is particularly strong. Joseph Conrad wrote about it: 'it is experience pushed a little (and only very little) beyond the actual facts of the case for the perfectly legitimate ... purpose of bringing it home to the minds and bosoms of the readers'. Since Joseph

Conrad's experience was very similar to Marlow's, it is worth recalling how he himself went to the Congo.

In 1889 Joseph Conrad was in much the same position as Marlow, having 'just returned to London after a lot of Indian Ocean, Pacific, China Seas – a regular dose of the East … and I was loafing about, hindering you fellows in your work and invading your homes, just as though I had got a heavenly mission to civilise you' (p. 22). He was in search of a command, and it may well be also that he saw a map in a shop window in Fleet Street and was reminded of his boyhood dreams of visiting the blank space in Central Africa, although by then 'It had become a place of darkness' (p. 22). Again, like Marlow, he 'set the women to work – to get a job' (p. 23) in the Congo – actually his aunt Marguerite Poradowska, who had connections with the 'Société Anonyme Belge pour le Commerce du Haut Congo'. The Congo Free State was at that time the personal property of King Léopold II of Belgium. The 'Société', though nominally independent, was administered by a collaborator of the King, Captain Albert Thys, to whom Joseph Conrad applied. His interview with Thys is briefly evoked in *Heart of Darkness* where the Captain is referred to as 'an impression of pale plumpness in a frock-coat' (p. 25). Joseph Conrad was appointed to replace a Captain Freiesleben (Fresleven in the novel).

He left from Bordeaux in the second week of May 1890 taking with him what he had written of *Almayer's Folly*. His impressions of his voyage down the coast have been recorded in *Heart of Darkness*. What is certain is that on the voyage out disillusionment was already setting in. He was appalled by what he discovered at the company's station at Matadi, as is clear from his creation of what he calls the 'grove of death' in the novel. In Marlow's walk to the Central Station he has also given a fairly close rendering of his own expedition, and, like Marlow, he found upon arrival that the boat he was to command, the *Florida*, had been sunk a few days before. He did not wait two months for the ship to be repaired, however, but sailed the next day on the *Roi des Belges* as second in command to Captain Koch, whom he relieved for a few days when the latter was ill.

The *Roi des Belges* travelled up-river to Stanley Falls in order to relieve an agent called Klein, who was seriously ill and (like Kurtz in *Heart of Darkness*) died on the way back. Kurtz was actually called Klein in the original draft (kurtz and klein mean 'short' and 'small' in German).

Whether the real agent served as a model for Kurtz or not matters less than the fact that he represented a type of white man frequently to be met in Africa at the time. Otto Lütken, a Danish captain who worked for eight years in the Congo and wrote approvingly of *Heart of Darkness* (though he pointed out that there were admirable white men in the Congo) had this to say about Kurtz: 'It is in the picture Joseph Conrad draws of Kurtz ... that his authorship rises supreme. The man is lifelike and convincing – heavens, how I know him! I have met one or two "Kurtzs" in my time in Africa, and I can see him now.'

Since the beginning of his voyage Joseph Conrad's isolation had grown, particularly on the *Roi des Belges*, for he did not get on at all with the company's acting director, Camille Delcommune. After his return to Kinshassa (the Central Station) he was preparing for a ten-month expedition to be led by Alexandre Delcommune, the director's brother but felt that the director might not keep the promise made to him in Brussels, that Joseph Conrad would command the boat on which the expedition was to leave. To his aunt he wrote at the time: 'Everything is repellent to me. Men and things; but especially men. And I too am repellent to them'. His health was also bad; he had discovered that fever and dysentery, rather than the romantic picture of exploration of his youth, was the more common lot of men in Africa. When he realised that he would not receive the command he returned home.

Joseph Conrad's four months in the Congo affected both his health and his outlook on life. Of course, they alone cannot be held responsible for Joseph Conrad's pessimism and gloomy disposition. He once said to his friend Edward Garnett 'Before the Congo I was a mere animal', by which he meant that he lacked the understanding of existence and the maturity every person ought to attain. His Congo experience put an end to his career as a sailor but made Joseph Conrad the artist.

OTHER WORKS BY JOSEPH CONRAD

When he gave up his work as a sailor, Joseph Conrad's adventures were all of the imagination. He wrote slowly, partly by temperament, partly because English was an acquired language; this also made for the unconventionality of his writing. Nevertheless, he produced thirty-one books and a large number of letters. In his early novels and stories, *The Nigger of the Narcissus*

(1897), *Lord Jim* (1900), and *Typhoon* (1903), he drew largely on his own experience at sea. This was soon after the first successes of Kipling (1865–1936) when interest in the remote parts of the Empire grew among British people. For a long time, however, Joseph Conrad's audience was limited, for he was more than a master of exotic scenes and narratives. The psychological complexity and technical subtleties of his stories sometimes put off his readers. He therefore lived modestly, but had a distinguished group of friends including H.G. Wells (1866–1946), John Galsworthy (1867–1933), and Ford Madox Ford (1873–1939) with whom he had endless discussions on literary technique. The two artists collaborated in the writing of two novels, *The Inheritors* (1901) and *Romance* (1902). With the great novels that followed his early period Joseph Conrad became a master of what is called 'indirect narration', which consists of presenting information in bits and pieces and from different points of view. *Nostromo* (1904) is the story of a revolution in a Latin-American republic and of a theft of a cargo of silver. This long and complex novel is closest to *Heart of Darkness* in that it also deals with imperialism and the gap between great humanitarian ideals and the failure to live up to them. It is a visionary novel in which Joseph Conrad prefigures the exploitation of populations, no longer by colonialism, but by a neo-colonialism supported by international capitalism. In *Nostromo* silver has the same corrupting effect as ivory in *Heart of Darkness*. *The Secret Agent* (1907) is based on the actual attempt of an anarchist to blow up Greenwich Observatory in 1894 in order to rouse British indignation against the Nihilists. In *Under Western Eyes* (1911), the most Slavic of his novels, Joseph Conrad created a memorable character in Razumov, a conspirator turned informer.

Success at last came to Joseph Conrad with a novel called *Chance* (1913), ironically not one of his best. His next novel, *Victory (*1915), has the same romantic tone as *Chance* and presents one of Joseph Conrad's favourite themes, emotional isolation. In *The Shadow-line* (1917), written in the symbolist manner of his early stories (like *The Secret Sharer*), he presents a positive character, the antithesis of many a negative personality in the earlier novels. Joseph Conrad's later books *The Rescue* (1920) and *The Rover* (1923) are generally considered as inferior to his best work.

Except for brief intervals when people reacted against imperialism, the history of Europe and of the countries conquered by Europeans between the fifteenth and the twentieth centuries was strongly influenced by the expansionism of England, France, the Netherlands, Portugal, Spain, and later Germany and Belgium, as well as by their determination to build empires overseas. Economic historians have demonstrated that the conquest of unexploited areas of the world by Britain in the latter half of the nineteenth century was the only way out of the economic depression of the 1880s. Others have argued that at the end of the nineteenth century the economic case for annexing large areas of jungle or desert was not convincing, but no European power was prepared to stand by while its rivals extended their territories. Imperialism was also vindicated on moral grounds, particularly by missionaries. It was considered as a means of liberating peoples from tyrannical rule or of bringing them the blessings of the Christian religion and of a supposedly superior civilisation. Most people at the end of the nineteenth century were sincerely convinced of this, and even as enlightened a man as George Bernard Shaw (1856–1950) could argue that 'if the Chinese [who actually had a longer cultural and commercial tradition than Britain] were incapable of establishing conditions in their own country which would promote peaceful commerce and civilised life, it was the duty of European powers to establish such conditions for them.'

The supporters of imperialism did not see it as a means of domination or exploitation. Lord Curzon (1859–1925), who was viceroy of India from 1898 to 1905, summed up their position clearly when he wrote: 'In empire, we have found not merely the key to glory and wealth, but the call to duty and the means of service to mankind'. Humanitarianism, a nineteenth-century movement concerned with human welfare, philanthropic activities and social reform, supported imperialism and sometimes exerted sufficient pressure to turn colonial concessions into enlightened centres, yet reacted against it when it turned out to be mere exploitation. By the end of the century, however, disillusionment prevailed as a result of the discrepancy between humanitarian ideals and the reality of colonial exploitation.

Nothing illustrates this more clearly than the colonisation of the Congo, which was part of the 'scramble for Africa'. In 1875 less than one-tenth of Africa had been turned into European colonies. By 1895 only one-tenth was not under European control. In the early 1880s several European powers, and the Belgian King Léopold II acting in his private capacity, were trying to control the Congo river basin peopled by independent tribal groups. The largest of them formed a kingdom called Congo and gave its name to the river. Léopold II became interested in Central Africa, at that time still a blank on the map, because he believed in his country's absolute need for a colony though he had the support of neither his government nor the Belgian people. For the purposes of exploration he founded the International Association for the Exploration and Civilisation of Africa, probably 'the International Society for the Suppression of Savage Customs' (p. 66) in *Heart of Darkness*. In 1877 came the news that the British journalist and explorer Henry M. Stanley (1841–1904) had travelled across Africa over a period of three years. The British government were not interested in developing the Congo, and in 1878 Stanley entered the service of Léopold II. From 1879 to 1884 Stanley was in the Congo basin where he opened up the country, launched steamers on the upper river and established a chain of stations along the river up to Stanley Falls. At the end of the Berlin Conference (from November 1884 to February 1885), which had met to define a free-trade zone in Central Africa but actually dealt with the partition of Africa and the establishment of zones of influence, the Congo was recognised as an 'independent state' and became the Congo Free State under the personal sovereignty of King Léopold.

The King subsidised the State, sometimes with the help of Belgium. Financial problems were solved by the establishment of the *régime domanial*, by which all vacant land as well as its products, mainly ivory and rubber, were declared State property. It killed all private trade and soon made the State very prosperous. It was soon alleged that the compulsory collection of rubber led to bad treatment of the native population. Specific charges were made by the British Consul in Boma, Roger Casement (1864–1916), in a report published in 1904 by the British government. It led to a strong anti-Congolese campaign and the foundation of the Congo Reform Association. A commission of inquiry was sent to the Congo, which confirmed the existence of grave abuses. Although efforts were made to improve the situation, a complete change could only be imposed by transferring control to the State of Belgium. In spite of strong opposition by the socialists and some liberals, the Congo was officially annexed by Belgium on 15 November 1908.

PART SIX

CRITICAL HISTORY

Joseph Conrad's hope that the resonance of his novel would hang in the air long after the last note had been struck has been more than fulfilled, largely because of its continuing relevance to humanity's experience in the twentieth century in both individual and political spheres. When it first appeared, however, it received mixed critical reactions. Some readers were puzzled by it or praised it for the wrong reasons, and it was only gradually that critics found ever new possibilities of interpretation. But Edward Garnett (1865–1937), the man of letters who 'discovered' Joseph Conrad, called it a 'psychological masterpiece', and in his excellent review focused on the novel's essential meaning: 'an analysis of the white man's morale when let loose from European restraint, and planted down in the tropics as an "emissary of light" armed to the teeth to make trade profits out of subject races'. However, as late as 1936 E.M. Forster found *Heart of Darkness* obscure as did F.R. Leavis in *The Great Tradition* (1948). Nevertheless, the novel's originality in both form and content was giving rise to a '*Heart of Darkness* tradition', in which other novelists follow in Joseph Conrad's footsteps, not just in Africa but in other parts of the world where similar experiences could have taken place or inspired similar imagined ventures.

CREATIVE RESPONSES TO HEART OF DARKNESS

Among fairly early 'affiliated' works one can name André Gide's *Voyage to the Congo* (1929), Graham Greene's *Journey Without Maps* (1936), Nadine Gordimer's *The Congo River* (1961) or even Hannah Arendt's philosophic treatise *Imperialism* (1951). Nevertheless, it is in the post-independence/**post-colonial** literatures that one finds the largest number of 're-writings' of *Heart of Darkness*, i.e. novels dealing with a similar subject but from a different, frequently opposite, point of view, that of the colonised who in Africa remained such an enigma to Joseph Conrad. To paraphrase Salman Rushdie's famous statement, 'the Empire writes back', these novels 'write back' to the canonical *Heart of Darkness*.

Among such works, one can name Wilson Harris's *Palace of the Peacock* (1960), *A Fringe of Leaves* (1976) by the Australian Nobel Prize winner Patrick White, Margaret Atwood's *Surfacing* (1976), Ishmael Reed's *Flight to Canada* (1976) and more recently David Dabydeen's *The Intended* (1991), a title clearly inspired by Kurtz's fiancée, as well as Timothy Findley's *Head Hunter* (1993). African writers have, of course, responded to *Heart of Darkness*, some of them very negatively (see below). The Kenyan novelist Ngugi Wa Thiong'o, whose reaction to the novel is ambivalent, has nevertheless acknowledged Joseph Conrad's influence on his own writing (see Peter Nazareth, *Conrad's Descendants*, 1990). However, the novelists who feel closest to Joseph Conrad in their approach to Africa are the Trinidadian writers V.S. Naipaul and his brother Shiva. V.S. Naipaul located two works of fiction in Africa, *In a Free State* (1971) and *A Bend in the River* (1979), which takes place in Mobutu's Zaïre and is a follow-up to *Heart of Darkness*. Both he and his brother Shiva (in *North of South: An African Journey*, 1979) transfer the nihilism, inefficiency and destructiveness of the 'pilgrims' of *Heart of Darkness* to the Africans and present a generally pessimistic, even negative view of the continent. However, Peter Nazareth, himself a novelist, argues that the Naipauls misunderstand both Joseph Conrad's political vision and his language (Peter Nazareth, *Out of Darkness*, 1982). Thus even for writers, Joseph Conrad's vision remains controversial.

It is worth pointing out that *Heart of Darkness* has been adapted to a different artistic medium in the now famous film by Francis Ford Coppola, *Apocalypse Now*. The action has been displaced to Vietnam at the time of the Vietnam war in which the Americans were the invaders. Much of the film reproduces Joseph Conrad's text literally.

CRITICAL APPROACHES

Heart of Darkness has received and continues to receive as much if not more critical attention than any work of fiction in English. It can even be said that the criticism of this novella illustrates the history of criticism in the twentieth century since most critical approaches have been applied to it: from the 'new criticism' (the expression by which it is known) that emerged in the 1920s but was dominant in the 1940s and 1950s, the 'moral formalism' that prevailed in England in the 1930s to the 1970s under the influence of F.R. Leavis, down to the latest contemporary critical theories, to which must be added the considerable but varied responses from a **post-colonial** perspective.

Albert Guerard in *Conrad the Novelist* (Harvard University Press, 1958) develops Edward Garnett's perception of *Heart of Darkness* as a 'psychological masterpiece'. He was the first critic to see in the narrative 'a journey into the self' and 'a dream of self-discovery'. Thomas Moser's *Joseph Conrad: Achievement and Decline* (Harvard University Press, 1957) puts forward a similar emphasis on the process of self-knowledge but also points out that the novel criticises European imperialism and racism, a view later questioned by some post-colonial critics. The 'new critics' and 'formalists' who were mainly concerned with the formal features of the novel to the exclusion of the context in which it was written, praised its artistic form and unity. This was Leo Gurko's approach in *Joseph Conrad: Giant and Exile* (Macmillan, 1962), though he also expressed the now unfashionable view that both imperialism and Marlow's lie to the Intended are redeemed by a 'benevolent and idealistic motivation'. Not so Avrom Fleishman who argued in *Conrad's Politics* (Johns Hopkins University Press, 1967) that Joseph Conrad was aware of the disruptive effects of imperialism.

A different critical perspective is offered in the many essays that use a psychoanalytical approach inspired either by Sigmund Freud or Carl Gustav Jung's analytical models. Among those is an influential chapter entitled 'Joseph Conrad's Uneasiness – and Ours' in Frederick Crews's *Out of My System: Psychoanalysis, Ideology, and Critical Methodology* (Oxford University Press, 1975). It was followed by a number of psychological or psycho-analytical readings such as Catharine Rising's *Darkness at Heart: Father and Sons in Conrad* (Greenwood Press, 1990) and Barry Stampfl's 'Marlow's Rhetoric of (Self-) Deception in *Heart of Darkness*' (1991) as well as Eugene Goodheart's *Desire and its Discontents* (Columbia University Press, 1991), the last two showing that the psychological and political aspects are intertwined.

Yet another approach is that of feminist critics who take Joseph Conrad to task for excluding women from the man's world he presents and especially for Marlow's lie to the Intended. Nina Pelikan Straus (1987) goes so far as to say that the woman who identifies with Marlow 'court[s] self-degradation'. Bette London (1989) writes that gender and race are 'inter-locking systems' and that Joseph Conrad presents both a racial and a gender ideology. If Africa is a continent from which European women like the Intended are excluded, then Kurtz's African mistress is less than a woman. Feminist criticism is one of several types of interpretation based on contemporary theories. You will find a good example of it in the edition of *Heart of Darkness* these notes refer to as well as sample essays illustrating various theoretical models together with a clear and excellent introduction to the theories themselves. In addition to the feminist approach already mentioned, these include 'reader-response criticism' based on the notion that, through his/her response to the text, the reader is an active maker who participates in the action presented by the text and its implications. '**Deconstruction**', a practice inspired by the writings of the French philosopher Jacques Derrida, 'deconstructs' or 'decenters' basic concepts or values that have always been central to Western philosophy like 'being', 'truth', 'God' or 'fatherland', though Derrida insists that one can never wholly escape the system one is trying to deconstruct. It is easy to see that this theory would appeal to post-colonial readers who try to 'decon-struct' the ideology of imperialism. 'New historicism', like the theoretical approaches already mentioned is part of a more general theoretical approach called '**post-structuralist**'. (The more advanced students can consult Ross C. Murfin's explanations on this subject in his edition of *Heart of Darkness*, or Selden and Widdowson's *A Reader's Guide to Contemporary Literary Theory*, Harvester Wheatsheaf, 1993.) Contrary to the 'new critics' and 'formalists' who tended to ignore the cultural conditions in which a text was created, the new historicists give it a primary importance. They argue that a text is necessarily interconnected with, and even a product of, the various aspects, social, political, cultural, of a particular society. The last essay in Murfin's edition is inspired by 'cultural criticism', which takes into account all aspects of culture, both 'high' and 'low' and denies the existence of a hierarchy between them. Cultural criticism is interdisciplinary and mixes approaches developed in various disciplines. Like the theories already mentioned, it is strongly influenced by Marxism.

Finally, the critical response of post-colonial writers and critics or of scholars who write from their perspective is, I would suggest, among the most important because they emerge from the very non-European people(s) Joseph Conrad wrote about in *Heart of Darkness* and most of his

other works. A representative selection of their response is to be found in
Robert D. Hamner, ed., *Joseph Conrad: Third World Perspectives* (Three
Continents Press, 1990).

POST-COLONIAL CRITICISM

In a tightly-argued, well-known article, 'An Image of Africa' (1977), the
Nigerian novelist Chinua Achebe initiated a now impressive list of what
post-colonial theorists call **'counter-discursive'** or 'resistant' readings of
Heart of Darkness. Commenting on the derogatory images of Africans in
the novel, Achebe concludes that Joseph Conrad was 'a bloody racist' and
that his book 'parades in the most vulgar fashion prejudices and insults
from which a selection of mankind has suffered untold agonies and
atrocities in the past and continues to do so in many ways and many places
today. I am talking about a story in which the very humanity of black
people is called in question' (in Hamner, pp. 124 and 126). Achebe's essay
seems to have served as a catalyst and released sharp criticism on Joseph
Conrad's 'imperialism'. Edward Said, who had formerly written on Joseph
Conrad in balanced terms (admittedly, on the formal aspects of *Heart of
Darkness*), is far more condemnatory in *Culture and Imperialism* (Vintage,
1993) as, for example, in the following statements: 'Marlow repeats and
confirms Kurtz's action: restoring Africa to European hegemony by
historizing and narrating its strangeness' (p. 198); or 'the startling purity of
the imperial quest in *Heart of Darkness* – when Marlow acknowledges that
he always felt a passion to fill in the great blank spaces on the map –
remains an overwhelming reality, a constitutive reality, in the culture of
imperialism' (p. 201).

Other critics, however, have qualified their reservations. Frances B.
Singh, for instance, agrees with Achebe that 'Marlow's ethnocentricity
leads him to side with the colonisers against the Africans' but concludes
that the 'colonialistic bias of *Heart of Darkness* ... reveals the limitations of
Joseph Conrad's notions rather than the existence of a reactionary and racist
streak in him' (in Kimbrough, *Heart of Darkness*, Norton, 1988, p. 280).
C.P. Sarvan points out that Joseph Conrad reflects to some extent the
attitudes of his age but finds that the emphasis in the presentation of men,
white and black, is on continuity and therefore on the 'fundamental oneness
of man and his nature' (in Kimbrough, p. 283).

Through her analysis of the formal aspects of *Heart of Darkness*, Benita Parry stresses its equivocal nature and argues that, while denouncing the infamous assumptions that underpin imperialism, Joseph Conrad simultaneously vindicates its idealistic intent and concludes his narrative with an affirmation of loyalty to Europe's 'illusory pure form' (*Parry, Conrad and Imperialism*, 1983). DCRA Goonetilleke (1990) demonstrates that Joseph Conrad's condemnation of colonialism is general and not limited to its Belgian version. He points to Marlow's limited understanding of his experience and power of analysis and, unlike many other critics, considers that Kurtz, not Marlow, is the main character. He concludes that Joseph Conrad was prescient in foreshadowing the collapse of civilisation.

In answer to Achebe's essay, the Guyanese novelist Wilson Harris wrote an imaginative vindication of *Heart of Darkness*. He calls it a 'frontier novel', by which he means that Joseph Conrad arrived upon a frontier of imagination which he never crossed, though to reach it in his time was an extraordinary achievement. Harris shows that the monolithic views that prevailed when Joseph Conrad wrote are disrupted by his language, by the 'qualitative and infinite variations of substance' (in Hamner, 1990, p.165) conveyed by the imagery in his novel. Through these images Joseph Conrad went a considerable way towards recognising the 'otherness' of the African people and broke with the 'uniform prejudice' that prevailed at the turn of the twentieth century. Peter Nazareth generally agrees with Harris, though he vindicates Joseph Conrad's novel more unreservedly and criticises both Achebe and Naipaul for not paying enough attention to words and therefore misinterpreting *Heart of Darkness*. (His article is also included in Hamner's collection of essays.) Finally, in 'The Creature of the Blue Lagoon' (1990), Michael Gilkes, another Guyanese writer, argues that Kurtz's cry 'comes from the discovery that the "savage" black woman and the "saintly" white woman are indivisible; sexual counterparts that emerge out of a process of social and cultural conditioning, the result of a fear of, and a fascination with, the Terrible Woman'. Joseph Conrad thus tacitly admitted the 'Fear of the Female that underlies the ethic of Patriarchalism' and attempted to maintain the lie of male supremacy (in Davis and Maes-Jelinek, eds, *Crisis and Creativity in the New Literatures in English*, p. 56).

PART SEVEN

Broader perspectives

Further reading

Background reading

Jocelyn Baines, *Joseph Conrad, A Critical Biography*, Weidenfeld & Nicholson, 1960; also Penguin Books, 1971

> The standard biography of Conrad. Contains an informative chapter on the 'Congo episode' in Conrad's life, an analysis of *Heart of Darkness* and of Marlow's role in Conrad's stories

Norman Sherry, *Conrad's Western World*, Cambridge University Press, 1971

> Offers a detailed discussion of the sources of *Heart of Darkness*, *Nostromo* and *The Secret Agent*. Contains many interesting and relevant illustrations

Norman Sherry, ed., *Conrad: The Critical Heritage,* Routledge, 1973

> Includes critical essays on Conrad's work from the first critical reactions to approximately the time of publication of this collection

Studies of *Heart of Darkness*

Chinua Achebe, 'An Image of Africa', *Research in African Literatures*, 9 (Spring 1978), pp. 1–15. Reprinted in Hamner (see below), pp. 119–29

> Presents a sharp criticism of Conrad's 'racism', arguing that the inferiority of Africans is taken for granted

Frederick Crews, *Out of my System: Psychoanalysis, Ideology, and Critical Methodology*, Oxford University Press, 1975

> Applies a Freudian reading to *Heart of Darkness*, arguing that it can be the expression of an Oedipus complex

Avrom Fleishman, *Conrad's Politics*, Johns Hopkins University Press, 1967

> Concentrates on the disruptive effects of imperialism on native society in *Heart of Darkness*

Michael Gilkes, 'The Creature of the Blue Lagoon', in Geoffrey Davis and Hena Maes-Jelinek, eds, *Crisis and Creativity in the New Literatures in English*, CROSS/CULTURES, 1, Amsterdam: Rodopi, 1990, pp. 46–60

Eugene Goodheart, *Desire and its Discontents*, Columbia University Press, 1991

> Argues that even politics are the outcome of desire and that reason and passion combine to motivate the white man's will-to-power

DCRA Goonetilleke, *Joseph Conrad. Beyond Culture and Background*, Macmillan, 1990

> Presents a balanced view of all aspects of *Heart of Darkness* which he sees mainly as a serious commentary on imperialism. Unlike many other critics, he does not think that Marlow is a reliable self-dramatization of Conrad but is implicitly criticised

Lawrence Graver, *Conrad's Short Fiction*, University of California Press, 1969

> The section on *Heart of Darkness* contains a good discussion of the frame in that novel

Albert Guerard, *Conrad the Novelist*, Harvard University Press, 1958

> Remains one of the best studies on Conrad. First presented *Heart of Darkness* as a 'night journey'

Leo Gurko, *Joseph Conrad: Giant in Exile*, Macmillan, 1962

> Pays close attention to the form and unity of *Heart of Darkness*

Robert D. Hamner, *Joseph Conrad: Third World Perspectives*, Washington, D.C.: Three Continents Press, 1990

> A very useful collection of essays, mostly though not exclusively, by post-colonial writers and critics, on Conrad's fictionalization of the colonised peoples

Wilson Harris, 'The Frontier on which *Heart of Darkness* Stands', in *Explorations* (Aarhus: Dangaroo Press, 1981, pp. 134–41). Reprinted in Hamner (p. 161–7) and in Kimbrough (pp. 280–5)

> Argues that Conrad was ahead of his time in disrupting monolithic imperialism through his imagery but was still partly limited by the prejudices of his time and did not cross the frontier towards a completely new vision

Robert Kimbrough, ed., *Heart of Darkness*, A Norton Critical Edition, Norton & Company, 3rd edition, 1988

> Apart from the text of *Heart of Darkness*, includes sections by various authors on 'Backgrounds and Sources', 'Writing the Story', 'Conrad on Life and Art', and 'Criticism'

F.R. Leavis, *The Great Tradition*, Chatto and Windus, 1948. Reprinted Peregrine Books, 1962

> A study of the writers who make up the 'great tradition' of English fiction, Jane Austen, Charles Dickens, George Eliot, Henry James and Joseph Conrad. It was considered for a long time as the major reference work as to what constituted the best fiction fit to be included in the **'canon'**

Bette London, 'Reading Race and Gender in Conrad's Dark Continent', *Criticism* 31 (1989), pp. 235–52

> A feminist essay which sees gender and race as part of Conrad's patriarchal and racial ideology which the narrative considers as 'self-evident'

Thomas Moser, *Joseph Conrad: Achievement and Decline*, Harvard University Press, 1957

> Considers that the major theme of *Heart of Darkness* is self-knowledge. He prefigures reader-response criticism by stating that Marlow's quest for self-knowledge must be paralleled by the reader's

Ross C. Murfin, ed., *Heart of Darkness*, Case Studies in Contemporary Criticism, Bedford Books of St Martin's Press, 2nd edition, 1996

> In addition to the text, presents critical essays all inspired by a **post-structuralist** theory, each preceded by a very useful description of the theory. Two essays in the first edition (1989) have been replaced by new ones

Peter Nazareth, 'Out of Darkness: Conrad and Other Third World Writers', *Conradiana*, xiv/3, 1982, pp. 173–87. Reprinted in Hamner, pp. 217–31

Peter Nazareth, 'Conrad's Descendants', *Conradiana*, xxii/2, 1990, pp. 101–9

Robert Nixon, *London Calling. V.S. Naipaul, Postcolonial Mandarin*, Oxford University Press, 1992

> Discusses the *Heart of Darkness* tradition and Conrad's influence on V.S. Naipaul

Benita Parry, *Conrad and Imperialism: Ideological Boundaries and Visionary Frontiers*, Macmillan, 1983
> Argues that Conrad's approach to imperialism in *Heart of Darkness* is ambivalent and presents two irreconcilable orders

Catharine Rising, *Darkness at Heart: Fathers and Sons in Conrad*, New York: Greenwood Press, 1990
> Widens Crews's thesis on Conrad's alleged oedipal complex by suggesting that the oedipal rivalry could involve an older, illustrious man who surpasses the father figure

Edward Said, *Joseph Conrad and the Fiction of Autobiography*, Harvard University Press, 1966
> Examines the connection between Conrad's life and his short fiction. Quotes in full Conrad's letter to his friend R.B. Cunninghame Graham's on *Heart of Darkness*

Edward Said, *The World, the Text and the Critic*, Faber and Faber, 1984 (1st American edition, 1983)
> One chapter 'Conrad: the Presentation of Narrative' examines the narrative technique in *Heart of Darkness*

Edward Said, *Culture and Imperialism*, 1st published 1993, Vintage, 1994
> Discusses *Heart of Darkness* occasionally to illustrate his thesis on cultural imperialism

C.P. Sarvan, 'Racism and the *Heart of Darkness*', *The International Fiction Review*, 7, 1 (1980), pp. 6–10. Reprinted in Kimbrough (pp. 280–5)
> Writes that Conrad reflected to some extent the attitudes of his age and pointed to the gap between technological progress in London and Africa. But his criticism of imperialism must not be underrated

Raman Selden and Peter Widdowson, *A Reader's Guide to Contemporary Literary Theory*, Harvester Wheatsheaf, 3rd edition, 1993
> Will help the more advanced student to understand the theoretical approaches to *Heart of Darkness*

Frances B. Singh, 'The Colonialistic Bias of *Heart of Darkness*', *Conradiana*, 10, (1978), pp. 41–54. Reprinted in Kimbrough, pp. 268–80
> Conrad was aware of some, though not of all, limitations in Marlow. Hence some contradictions in the text which reveal Conrad's limited understanding of some of the notions he uses

LITERARY TERMS continued

Barry Stampfl, 'Marlow's Rhetoric of (Self-)Deception in *Heart of Darkness*', *Modern Fiction Studies* 37, (1991), pp. 183–96

Analyses Freudian repressions in Marlow's narrative through a close examination of the syntax in his narrative

Nina Pelikan Straus, 'The Exclusion of the Intended from Secret Sharing in Conrad's *Heart of Darkness*', *Novel: A Forum of Fiction*, 20, (1987), pp. 123–37

A feminist essay which argues that the artistic conventions of *Heart of Darkness* are 'brutally sexist' (p. 125)

World events	Joseph Conrad	Literary events
1482 Portuguese navigator Diogo Cam visits the mouth of the Congo		
	1857 Born of Polish parents in Berdychev, Poland, now in Ukraine	
1863 Polish Uprising	**1863** Conrad's father arrested and exiled north of Moscow	
	1865 Mother dies	
	1869 Father dies, placed under care of his uncle	
	1874 Travels to Marseilles and begins life as a sailor on a French vessel	
1876-7 Henry M. Stanley travels the Lualaba-Congo river system to its mouth		
1878 King Léopold II of Belgium founds the International Association of Africa; Stanley enters service of Léopold II	**1878** Attempts suicide	**1878** Henry M. Stanley, *Through the Dark Continent*
1879-84 Stanley begins opening of Congo Basin to colonists, launching steamers and establishing stations on upper river	**1879** First visits England	**1880** Guy de Maupassant, *Boule de Suif* **1883** Robert Louis Stevenson, *Treasure Island*
1884 The Berlin Conference establishes the Congo Free State, open to trade of all nations, and outlaws the slave trade		
1885 Congo Free State is placed under the personal sovereignty of Léopold II		
	1886 Becomes a British subject and master marriner	**1886** Thomas Hardy, *The Mayor of Casterbridge* **1888** Rudyard Kipling, *Plain Tales from the Hills*
	1890 Visits the Belgian Congo	**1890** Henry M. Stanley, *In Darkest Africa*
	1894 Settles in England	
	1895 Publishes his first novel, *Almayer's Folly*	
	1896 Marries Jessie George	
	1897 *The Nigger of the Narcissus*	

World events	Joseph Conrad	Literary events
	1900 *Lord Jim*	
	1901 *The Inheritors* (with Ford Maddox Ford)	**1901** Rudyard Kipling, *Kim*
	1902 *Heart of Darkness*	
	1903 *Romance* (with Ford Maddox Ford), *Typhoon*	
1904 Report of commission reveals widespread abuses against native inhabitants	**1904** *Nostromo*	
1904-8 Léopold's attempts to stop abuses are unsuccessful	**1907** *The Secret Agent*	**1907-8** Ford Maddox Ford, *Fifth Queen* trilogy
1908 The Congo becomes a Belgian colony		
	1911 *Under Western Eyes*	
	1912 Publishes his autobiography, *A Personal Record*	
	1913 Publishes his first popular and financial success, *Chance*	
	1915 *Victory*	
	1917 *The Shadow Line*	
	1919 *The Arrow of Gold*	
	1920 *The Rescue*	
	1923 *The Rover*	
	1924 Dies of a heart attack at Bishopsbourne near Canterbury	
	1925 His final, unfinished novel, *Suspense* is published posthumously	
		1929 André Gide, *Voyage to the Congo*
		1936 Graham Greene, *Journey without Maps*
		1951 Hannah Arendt, *Imperialism*
1960 Belgian rule ends and the Republic of the Congo is established		
		1961 Nadine Gordimer, *The Congo River*
		1979 V.S. Naipaul, *A Bend in the River*

canon a term originally applied to the books of the Bible accepted as genuine by the Christian Church. It has come to be applied to literary works considered as 'the best' in a given culture. The concept as such is now questioned by literary critics who challenge the criteria by which a work is thought worthy to be included in the canon

counter-discursive a type of criticism that reacts against the usually accepted 'discourse', taken for granted but actually a mere 'construct' of its author (see post-structuralism)

deconstruction one the critical theories strongly influenced by the French philosopher Jacques Derrida, in a post-structuralist approach to literature. It argues that no text has a final, absolute meaning sustained by terms which have always operated as centering principles in Western philosophy, like 'being', 'essence,' 'God', etc. The result is a 'decentering' of these notions, though Derrida also asserts that one can never dislodge them completely from one's argumentation

flashforward the reverse of a flashback, that is, a jump ahead in time to a later period in the story

leitmotif a recurring phrase, theme or image in a text

mise-en-abyme a French term first used with regard to André Gide's *The Counterfeiters*, a novel whose main character is himself working on a novel similar to the main narrator's story. It implies that meaning can be repeatedly deferred

post-colonialism refers to all aspects of political, social and cultural life, including language and literature, in post-independence, post-colonial countries. With reference to literature, the term is often used to describe all writings from the beginning of colonisation and not just post-independence works. It is now used in preference to 'Commonwealth' literature or even 'New Literatures in English'

post-structuralism covers a number of theoretical approaches to language and literature which have developed out of, while also reacting against, structuralism. It argues that the meaning of words is neither fixed nor absolute but varies with the context and thought patterns in which they are used. Therefore narratives do not have stable, absolute referents or 'centres' like 'being', 'God', etc. (see deconstruction). They are so many forms of 'discourse', that is, subjective constructs of a given culture, period and subjective elements

self-reflexive describes a text, referring to, and reflecting on, its own process of writing and meaning

See also the glossary in Ross C. Murfin's edition of *Heart of Darkness* and Martin Gray, *A Dictionary of Literary Terms*, Longman, York Press, 1992

AUTHOR OF THIS NOTE

Hena Maes-Jelinek OBE, is honorary professor of English and Commonwealth literature of the University of Liège. Her books include *Criticism of Society in the English Novel between the Wars, The Naked Design, Wilson Harris, Wilson Harris: the Uncompromising Imagination* (ed.). She has edited ten books of critical essays on post-colonial literatures and published widely in that field, specialising in Australian and Caribbean fiction, particularly Wilson Harris's work. She co-edits the series CROSS/CULTURES: *Readings in the Post/Colonial Literatures in English* published by Rodopi (Amsterdam/Atlanta).

Notes

NOTES

Notes

Notes

NOTES

Notes

York Notes Advanced (£3.99 each)

Margaret Atwood
The Handmaid's Tale

Jane Austen
Emma

Jane Austen
Pride and Prejudice

William Blake
Songs of Innocence and of Experience

Charlotte Brontë
Jane Eyre

Emily Brontë
Wuthering Heights

Geoffrey Chaucer
The Wife of Bath's Prologue and Tale

Joseph Conrad
Heart of Darkness

Charles Dickens
Great Expectations

F. Scott Fitzgerald
The Great Gatsby

Thomas Hardy
Tess of the d'Urbervilles

Seamus Heaney
Selected Poems

James Joyce
Dubliners

Arthur Miller
Death of a Salesman

William Shakespeare
Antony and Cleopatra

William Shakespeare
Hamlet

William Shakespeare
King Lear

William Shakespeare
The Merchant of Venice

William Shakespeare
Much Ado About Nothing

William Shakespeare
Othello

William Shakespeare
Romeo and Juliet

William Shakespeare
The Tempest

Mary Shelley
Frankenstein

Alice Walker
The Color Purple

Tennessee Williams
A Streetcar Named Desire

John Webster
The Duchess of Malfi

GCSE and equivalent levels (£3.50 each)

Harold Brighouse
Hobson's Choice

Charles Dickens
Great Expectations

Charles Dickens
Hard Times

George Eliot
Silas Marner

William Golding
Lord of the Flies

Thomas Hardy
The Mayor of Casterbridge

Susan Hill
I'm the King of the Castle

Barry Hines
A Kestrel for a Knave

Harper Lee
To Kill a Mockingbird

Arthur Miller
A View from the Bridge

Arthur Miller
The Crucible

George Orwell
Animal Farm

J.B. Priestley
An Inspector Calls

J.D. Salinger
The Catcher in the Rye

William Shakespeare
Macbeth

William Shakespeare
The Merchant of Venice

William Shakespeare
Romeo and Juliet

William Shakespeare
Twelfth Night

George Bernard Shaw
Pygmalion

John Steinbeck
Of Mice and Men

Mildred D. Taylor
Roll of Thunder, Hear My Cry

James Watson
Talking in Whispers

A Choice of Poets

Nineteenth Century Short Stories

Poetry of the First World War

Chinua Achebe
Things Fall Apart

Edward Albee
Who's Afraid of Virginia Woolf?

Maya Angelou
I Know Why The Caged Bird Sings

Jane Austen
Mansfield Park

Jane Austen
Northanger Abbey

Jane Austen
Persuasion

Jane Austen
Pride and Prejudice

Jane Austen
Sense and Sensibility

Samuel Beckett
Waiting for Godot

John Betjeman
Selected Poems

Robert Bolt
A Man for All Seasons

Charlotte Brontë
Jane Eyre

Emily Brontë
Wuthering Heights

Robert Burns
Selected Poems

Lord Byron
Selected Poems

Geoffrey Chaucer
The Franklin's Tale

Geoffrey Chaucer
The Knight's Tale

Geoffrey Chaucer
The Merchant's Tale

Geoffrey Chaucer
The Miller's Tale

Geoffrey Chaucer
The Nun's Priest's Tale

Geoffrey Chaucer
The Pardoner's Tale

Geoffrey Chaucer
Prologue to the Canterbury Tales

Samuel Taylor Coleridge
Selected Poems

Daniel Defoe
Moll Flanders

Daniel Defoe
Robinson Crusoe

Shelagh Delaney
A Taste of Honey

Charles Dickens
Bleak House

Charles Dickens
David Copperfield

Charles Dickens
Oliver Twist

Emily Dickinson
Selected Poems

John Donne
Selected Poems

Douglas Dunn
Selected Poems

George Eliot
Middlemarch

George Eliot
The Mill on the Floss

T.S. Eliot
The Waste Land

T.S. Eliot
Selected Poems

Henry Fielding
Joseph Andrews

E.M. Forster
Howards End

E.M. Forster
A Passage to India

John Fowles
The French Lieutenant's Woman

Elizabeth Gaskell
North and South

Oliver Goldsmith
She Stoops to Conquer

Graham Greene
Brighton Rock

Graham Greene
The Heart of the Matter

Graham Greene
The Power and the Glory

Willis Hall
The Long and the Short and the Tall

Thomas Hardy
Far from the Madding Crowd

Thomas Hardy
Jude the Obscure

Thomas Hardy
The Return of the Native

Thomas Hardy
Selected Poems

Thomas Hardy
Tess of the d'Urbervilles

L.P. Hartley
The Go-Between

Nathaniel Hawthorne
The Scarlet Letter

Seamus Heaney
Selected Poems

Ernest Hemingway
A Farewell to Arms

Ernest Hemingway
The Old Man and the Sea

Homer
The Iliad

Homer
The Odyssey

Gerard Manley Hopkins
Selected Poems

Ted Hughes
Selected Poems

Aldous Huxley
Brave New World

Henry James
Portrait of a Lady

Ben Jonson
The Alchemist

Ben Jonson
Volpone

James Joyce
A Portrait of the Artist as a Young Man

John Keats
Selected Poems

Philip Larkin
Selected Poems

D.H. Lawrence
The Rainbow

D.H. Lawrence
Selected Stories

D.H. Lawrence
Sons and Lovers

D.H. Lawrence
Women in Love

Louise Lawrence
Children of the Dust

FUTURE TITLES (continued)

Laurie Lee
Cider with Rosie

Christopher Marlowe
Doctor Faustus

John Milton
Paradise Lost Bks I & II

John Milton
Paradise Lost IV & IX

Robert O'Brien
Z for Zachariah

Sean O'Casey
Juno and the Paycock

George Orwell
Nineteen Eighty-four

John Osborne
Look Back in Anger

Wilfred Owen
Selected Poems

Harold Pinter
The Caretaker

Sylvia Plath
Selected Works

Alexander Pope
Selected Poems

Jean Rhys
Wide Sargasso Sea

Willy Russell
Educating Rita

Willy Russell
Our Day Out

William Shakespeare
As You Like It

William Shakespeare
Coriolanus

William Shakespeare
Henry IV Pt 1

William Shakespeare
Henry IV Pt II

William Shakespeare
Henry V

William Shakespeare
Julius Caesar

William Shakespeare
Measure for Measure

William Shakespeare
A Midsummer Night's Dream

William Shakespeare
Richard II

William Shakespeare
Richard III

William Shakespeare
Sonnets

William Shakespeare
The Taming of the Shrew

William Shakespeare
The Tempest

William Shakespeare
The Winter's Tale

George Bernard Shaw
Arms and the Man

George Bernard Shaw
Saint Joan

Richard Brinsley Sheridan
The Rivals

R.C. Sherriff
Journey's End

Rukshana Smith
Salt on the Snow

Muriel Spark
The Prime of Miss Jean Brodie

John Steinbeck
The Grapes of Wrath

John Steinbeck
The Pearl

R.L. Stevenson
Dr Jekyll and Mr Hyde

Tom Stoppard
Rosencrantz and Guildenstern are Dead

Jonathan Swift
Gulliver's Travels

Robert Swindells
Daz 4 Zoe

John Millington Synge
The Playboy of the Western World

W.M. Thackeray
Vanity Fair

Mark Twain
Huckleberry Finn

Virgil
The Aeneid

Derek Walcott
Selected Poems

Oscar Wilde
The Importance of Being Earnest

Tennessee Williams
Cat on a Hot Tin Roof

Tennessee Williams
The Glass Menagerie

Virginia Woolf
Mrs Dalloway

Virginia Woolf
To the Lighthouse

William Wordsworth
Selected Poems

W.B. Yeats
Selected Poems

Six Women Poets

York Notes – the Ultimate Literature Guides

York Notes are recognised as the best literature study guides.
If you have enjoyed using this book and have found it useful, you
can now order others directly from us – simply follow the ordering
instructions below.

HOW TO ORDER

Decide which title(s) you require and then order in one of the following
ways:

Booksellers
All titles available from good bookstores.

By post
List the title(s) you require in the space provided overleaf,
select your method of payment, complete your name and
address details and return your completed order form and
payment to:

Addison Wesley Longman Ltd
PO BOX 88
Harlow
Essex CM19 5SR

By phone
Call our Customer Information Centre on 01279 623923 to
place your order, quoting mail number: HEYN1.

By fax
Complete the order form overleaf, ensuring you fill in your
name and address details and method of payment, and fax it
to us on 01279 414130.

By e-mail
E-mail your order to us on awlhe.orders@awl.co.uk listing
title(s) and quantity required and providing full name and
address details as requested overleaf. Please quote mail
number: HEYN1. Please do not send credit card details by
e-mail.

York Notes Order Form

Titles required:

Quantity	Title/ISBN	Price

Sub total _____
Please add £2.50 postage & packing _____
(*P & P is free for orders over £50*) _____
Total _____

Mail no: HEYN1

Your Name _____

Your Address _____

_____

Postcode _____ Telephone _____

Method of payment

☐ I enclose a cheque or a P/O for £_____ made payable to Addison Wesley Longman Ltd

☐ Please charge my Visa/Access/AMEX/Diners Club card
Number _____ Expiry Date _____
Signature _____ Date _____

(please ensure that the address given above is the same as for your credit card)

Prices and other details are correct at time of going to press but may change without notice. All orders are subject to status.

☐ *Please tick this box if you would like a complete listing of Longman Study Guides (suitable for GCSE and A-level students)*

York Press

Longman

Addison Wesley Longman